PUB STROLLS IN OXFORDSHIRE

Roger Noyce

COUNTRYSIDE BOOKS
NEWBURY BERKSHIRE

First published 2003

COUNTRYSIDE BOOKS
3 Catherine Road
Newbury, Berkshire

To view our complete range of books,
please visit us at
www.countrysidebooks.co.uk

ISBN 1 85306 780 6

Designed by Graham Whiteman

Maps by the author
Photographs by Margaret Noyce

Typeset by Techniset Typesetters, Newton-le-Willows
Produced through MRM Associates Ltd., Reading
Printed by J.W. Arrowsmith Ltd., Bristol

Contents

INTRODUCTION 6

WALK

1 CROPREDY – The Red Lion (4 miles) 7

2 WROXTON – The North Arms (3¾ miles) 10

3 NORTH NEWINGTON – The Blinking Owl (2½ miles) 13

4 ADDERBURY – The Red Lion Hotel (3 miles) 16

5 HOOK NORTON – The Sun Inn (3 miles) 19

6 GREAT TEW – The Falkland Arms (3¾ miles) 22

7 FRINGFORD – The Butchers Arms (3 miles) 25

8 CHIPPING NORTON – The Chequers (2½ miles) 28

9 TACKLEY – The Gardiner Arms (3 miles) 31

10 CHARLBURY – The Bell Hotel (4 miles) 34

11 WOODSTOCK – The Black Prince (4 miles) 37

12 THRUPP – The Boat Inn (3 miles) 40

13 MURCOTT – The Nut Tree (4 miles) 43

14 SWINBROOK – The Swan Inn (2½ miles) 46

15 BECKLEY – The Abingdon Arms (4 miles) 49

16 MINSTER LOVELL – The Mill and Old Swan (3½ miles) 52

17 OXFORD – The Crown (1½ miles) 55

18 THAME – The Bird Cage Inn (3 miles) 58

19 STANTON HARCOURT – Harcourt Arms (2 miles) 61

AREA MAP SHOWING LOCATION OF THE WALKS

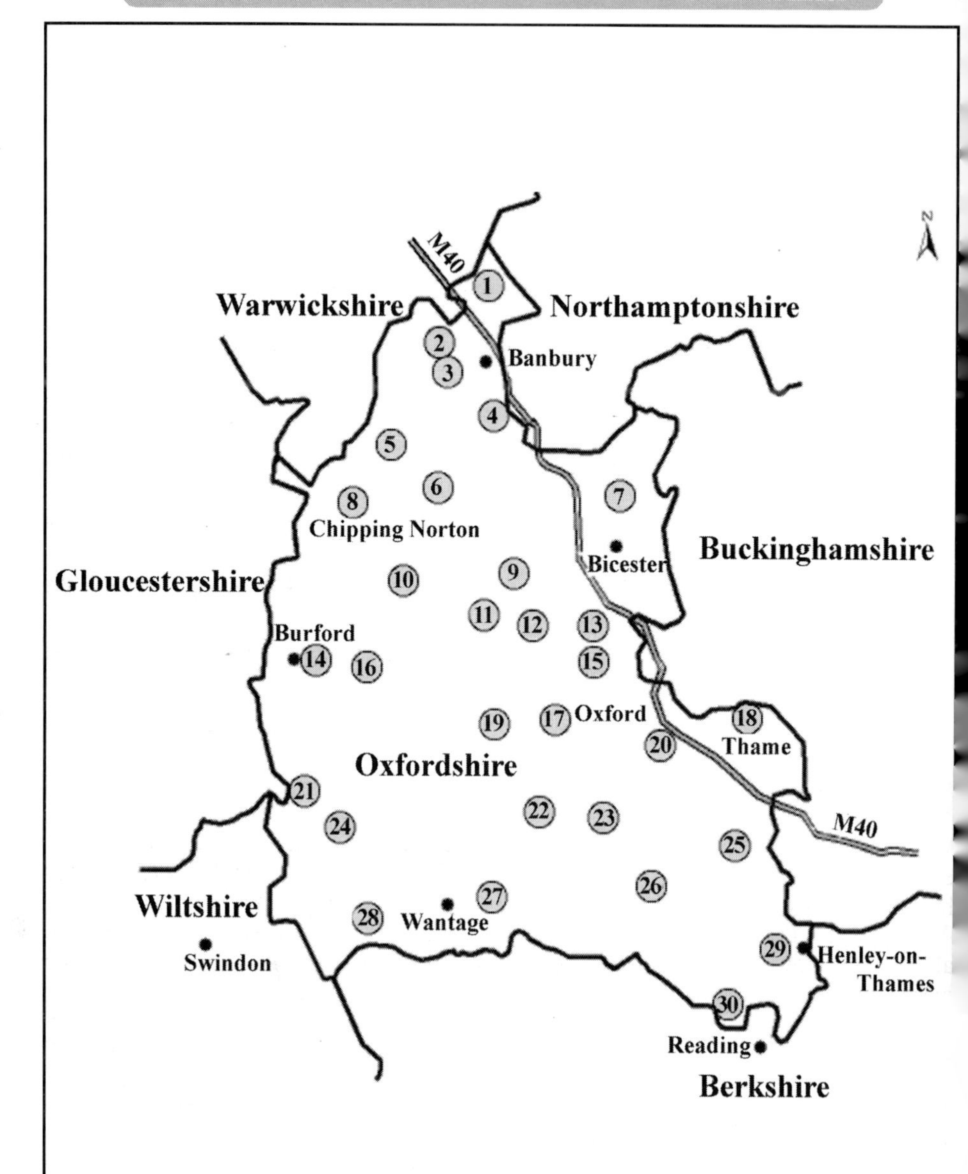

WALK

20 GREAT MILTON – The Bull ($2^3/_4$ miles) 64

21 KELMSCOTT – The Plough ($1^1/_2$ miles) 67

22 ABINGDON – The Nags Head on the Thames ($1^1/_2$ miles) 70

23 DORCHESTER – Fleur de Lys Inn ($2^1/_2$ miles) 73

24 FARINGDON – The Old Crown Coaching Inn (2 miles) 76

25 CHRISTMAS COMMON – The Fox & Hounds (3 miles) 79

26 WALLINGFORD – The Boathouse ($2^1/_2$ miles) 82

27 EAST HENDRED – The Wheatsheaf Inn (4 miles) 85

28 WOOLSTONE – The White Horse (4 miles) 88

29 ROTHERFIELD GREYS – The Maltsters Arms ($3^1/_2$ miles) 91

30 GORING HEATH – The King Charles Head (4 miles) 94

PUBLISHER'S NOTE

We hope that you obtain considerable enjoyment from this book; great care has been taken in its preparation. Although at the time of publication all routes followed public rights of way or permitted paths, diversion orders can be made and permissions withdrawn.

We cannot, of course, be held responsible for such diversion orders and any inaccuracies in the text which result from these or any other changes to the routes nor any damage which might result from walkers trespassing on private property. We are anxious though that all details covering the walks are kept up to date and would therefore welcome information from readers which would be relevant to future editions.

The simple sketch maps that accompany the walks in this book are based on notes made by the author whilst checking out the routes on the ground. They are designed to show you how to reach the start, to point out the main features of the overall circuit, and they contain a progression of numbers that relate to the paragraphs of the text.

However, for the benefit of a proper map, we do recommend that you purchase the relevant Ordnance Survey sheet covering your walk. The Ordnance Survey maps are widely available, especially through booksellers and local newsagents.

INTRODUCTION

Red kites soaring majestically over tree-covered hilltops; colourful narrow-boats making their way along the picturesque Oxford Canal; attractive villages of honey coloured stone with streets of thatched cottages; gentle hills inviting you to share their stunning views; and the magical River Thames offering a picture of modern leisure with boats of all shapes and sizes. These are a few of my favourite things that can be found in the historic county of Oxfordshire.

The 30 pub strolls in this book seek to explore Oxfordshire's feast of history, its amazing ancient buildings, its gentle rolling countryside, its fine hills and its warm welcome. Varying in length from 1½ to 4 miles, the walks can be enjoyed equally by those new to walking and regular walkers. In the beautiful city of Oxford you can admire its wonderful array of historic buildings, visit one of the finest universities in the UK and perhaps take a boat trip on the River Thames. In the villages around the county town, there are picture postcard pubs that form the base for pleasant walking. Stroll through the attractive Cotswold villages of Great Tew and North Newington, where thatched cottages line the streets. The walk at Woodstock leads you along public footpaths through the Great Park, where you can enjoy superb views of Blenheim Palace. Experience the sight of red kites soaring above Mapledurham as you stroll to visit a fine Elizabethan manor house, idyllically situated by the side of the river. At Dorchester upon Thames, the ancient abbey dominates the village and the walk takes you along the banks of the river past a number of beautiful thatched cottages. The short walk along the famous Ridgeway near Woolstone offers the opportunity to see possibly the oldest of Britain's chalk hill figures. The Oxford Canal was built in 1790 to link the River Thames with Midlands industry and you can saunter along the towpath at Cropredy.

The walking surface on the strolls is generally good so that persons of mature years and families with young children should have no difficulty. In dry weather, the paths will be firm underfoot and normal outdoor footwear should be adequate. In wet weather, or during the winter months, there could be moist stretches on some footpaths; then it is preferable to wear stout, waterproof boots or shoes.

There can be few greater pleasures in life than to combine a visit to a pub with a delightful country ramble, and to facilitate this, each walk either starts from an attractive pub or passes a named pub en route. Details of parking facilities are provided, together with information on the food and drinks available – the telephone number and e-mail address (where known) are included to enable you to make enquiries before your visit. For most of the strolls car parking is available at the pub for patrons but please be courteous and advise the landlord if you intend to leave your vehicle in the car park while you walk.

All of the routes incorporate public rights of way, where there is an onus upon every walker to always follow the Country Code, to look after our precious countryside and to protect the environment for future generations.

I am pleased to invite you to stroll along the lovely footpaths in the beautiful county of Oxfordshire and to visit some of its pubs and inns.

Roger Noyce

Cropredy
The Red Lion

MAP: OS EXPLORER 206 (GR SP:470464) | **WALK 1** | **DISTANCE:** 4 MILES

DIRECTIONS TO START: CROPREDY IS SITUATED 4½ MILES NORTH OF BANBURY. LEAVE BANBURY ON THE A361 TOWARDS DAVENTRY. JUST BEFORE REACHING THE VILLAGE OF WARDINGTON, GO LEFT DOWN A LANE SIGNPOSTED TO CROPREDY. **PARKING:** PARK IN THE LARGE CAR PARK ON THE LEFT JUST BEFORE YOU ARRIVE IN THE VILLAGE.

The fiercest battle of the Civil War was fought at Cropredy Bridge in 1644 when the Parliamentary troops, under General Waller, encountered the Royalist troops. During the fighting the villagers in Cropredy feared for their church and its treasures and hid a beautiful brass eagle lectern by dropping it into the River Cherwell for safe keeping. Fifty years later, the lectern was recovered but a lion foot was missing. This was replaced in bronze so that today the lectern has two brass feet and one bronze.

This stroll takes you from Cropredy along the banks of the lovely Oxford Canal, which was opened in 1790. Today, you will enjoy seeing a mixture of colourful narrow-boats pursuing their leisure activities. The route goes through the attractive village of Williamscott and over pastureland and returns to Cropredy along the canal towpath.

The Red Lion

There has been an ale house in Red Lion Street since 1540 and the thatched inn has been here since the 15th century. The pub is declared to be haunted by a man, a woman and a girl, whose footsteps can still be heard – they were slaughtered by a Roundhead soldier in the battle of Cropredy Bridge in 1644.

The Red Lion is open from 12 noon to 3 pm and from 6 pm to 11 pm every day of the week. Evening opening on Sunday is from 7 pm to 10.30 pm. Hook Norton, Wychwood Hobgoblin and Tetley ales are always available plus two guest ales. There is Scrumpy Jack to please the cider drinker and a wide selection of wines is also available. Food can be had between 12 noon and 2 pm and from 7 pm to 9 pm during the week and Sunday lunch between 12.30 pm and 2.30 pm – booking is advisable during the summer months. The inn does not serve food on Mondays during the winter. A wide selection of home made food is on offer and the home made sweets are a treat. You will enjoy a lovely meal in this historic pub, maybe tempted by the Beef Nom Pedra or perhaps the delicious Moussaka.

Children are allowed on the patio area. Dogs are not allowed in the pub. Telephone: 01295 750224.

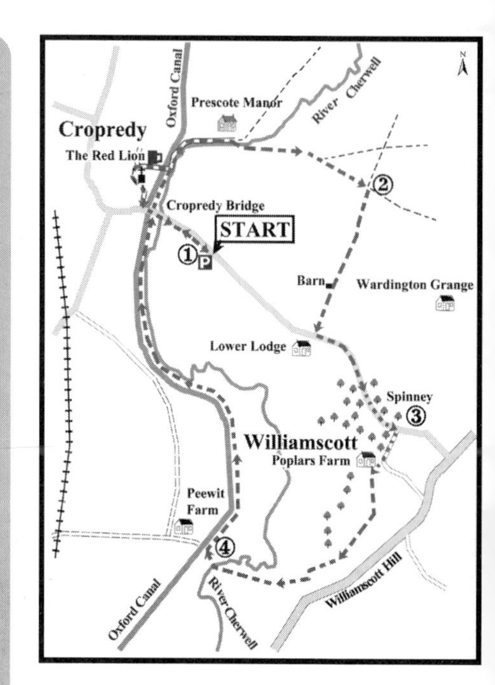

The Walk

① From the car park, go left towards Cropredy village. Just before Cropredy Bridge go right past the village shop and descend to the towpath of the Oxford Canal. A lovely view of the canal can be enjoyed as you progress northwards along the towpath. In 350 yards, go right over a stile into a lane and stroll along a farm drive by the side of the River Cherwell. After about 250 yards, when by the wall of Prescote Manor, go right over a farm bridge over the Cherwell and follow the direction of the waymark on the bridge, walking along the edge of fields until you reach a wide green track.

② Here, turn right and, passing a farm barn on your right, continue until you reach the road. Go left along the quiet road into the village of Williamscott.

③ Where the road bends gently left, go right, into the centre of the village. Just before you reach a telephone box, go right towards Poplars Farm, then bear left and stroll along the roadway to the farm buildings and into pastureland. The path arcs left and you ascend to a farm gate. Go

The Oxford Canal at Cropredy

right just before the gate and walk to the right of the field hedge. Proceed through the farm gate at the bottom of the field and continue over a couple more fields, aiming for a farm gate set about 50 yards to the left of a footbridge. A further footbridge over the River Cherwell leads to a bridge over the Oxford Canal.

④ Descend onto the towpath, turn right under the bridge and walk the pleasant canal towpath back to Cropredy. You will pass by several lock gates and may be lucky enough to see a heron or perhaps a fisherman catching a rudd or perch in the canal water. At canal bridge number 153 ascend to the road in Cropredy, cross over the canal to arrive in Red Lion Street, where you will find the Red Lion inn. To return to the car park, continue up Red Lion Street and enter the churchyard of St Mary the Virgin. Bear left around the church building and exit via a village footpath that leads back to Cropredy Bridge. The car park is on the right about 100 yards beyond the bridge.

PLACES OF INTEREST NEARBY

Sulgrave Manor (7 miles E) was the ancestral home of George Washington. Telephone: 01295 760205.

Wroxton

The North Arms

MAP: OS EXPLORER 191 (GR SP:414415)

WALK 2

DISTANCE: 3¾ MILES

DIRECTIONS TO START: WROXTON IS 3¼ MILES WEST OF BANBURY. LEAVE BANBURY ON THE A422, STRATFORD-UPON-AVON ROAD. GO LEFT INTO THE VILLAGE CENTRE AND PAST THE CHURCH TO ARRIVE BY THE NORTH ARMS. **PARKING:** CUSTOMERS MAY USE THE CAR PARK AT THE NORTH ARMS WHILE WALKING. PLEASE ASK FIRST.

This pleasant stroll will take you through the lovely village of Wroxton and past an obelisk and a fine college on the return route.

Wroxton is a small village with many mullioned, thatched cottages of brown stone. The village pond, which is the private residence of quite a few ducks, is surrounded by a delightful scene of peace and serenity. Wroxton College (a former Abbey) is undoubtedly the most famous building in the village. It is a fine 17th century gabled house built on the site of an Augustinian priory (1207), and houses three Holbeins and a superb Zucchero. Several mementoes of royalty remain in the building, including a quilt embroidered by Mary Queen of Scots. Wroxton College is occupied by Farleigh Dickinson University, USA and is not open to the public.

The North Arms

Built in the 17th century as cottages, the fine building was changed to a public house in 1850. The superb thatched inn has a thatched deer on its roof and a delightful south-facing garden.

Opening hours are from 12 noon to 2.30 pm and from 5.30 pm to 11 pm on weekdays; at weekends from 12 noon to 11 pm on Saturday and to 10.30 pm on Sunday. There is a good selection of beers and ciders – Greene King recently became the owners.

A wide selection of food is available between 12 noon and 2 pm and from 6.30 pm to 8.45 pm during the week, but all day at weekends, up to 8.45 pm on Saturday and 7.30 pm on Sunday. One can select lunches from snacks of soups and rolls to T-bone steak – these are popular with walkers, who will enjoy dining in the superb rear gardens amid colourful flowers – booking is advisable on all occasions but essential for Sunday lunch.

Children are allowed in the pub and in the garden seating area but dogs are only allowed in the garden and must be kept on a lead at all times. Telephone: 01295 730318.

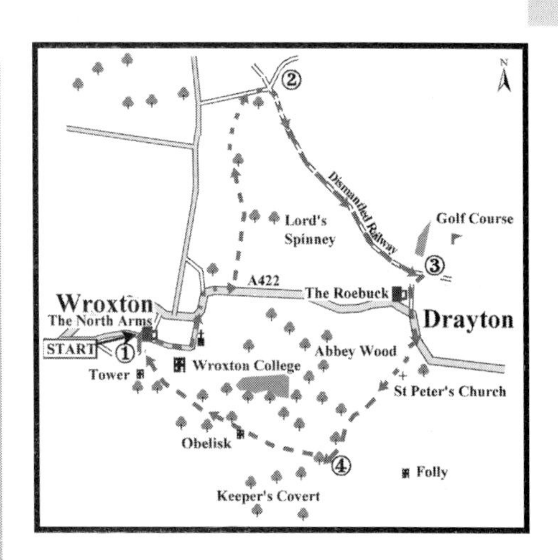

The Walk

① From the green in Wroxton, stroll along Church Street and this will take you left past the church and some delightful cottages to reach the corner of the A422 near to the Wroxton House Hotel. Go past this lovely building and you will pass by several other thatched cottages (note the very old thatched church of St Thomas of Canterbury on the right of the road) as you leave the village behind. Just after passing by the 30 mph sign, go left onto a clear footpath that proceeds northwards across the fields. The path will lead you past the edge of Lord's Spinney and you then ascend the next field to a height of 480 ft, from where there is a pleasing view of the village of Horley ahead of you. A gentle descent will take you through the edge of woodland until you arrive at a lane. Go right along the lane for 125 yards.

② Now turn right and walk down a clear footpath by the side of trees. This is the line of a dismantled railway and offers easy walking with glimpses of typical Oxfordshire countryside on either side. After walking the path for about 1,300 yards you will see a pool on your left and a golf course. Look out for a footpath that crosses the old railway.

③ Go right onto this footpath through meadowland into Queens' Avenue in the village of Drayton. Follow the pavement of the A422 and stroll through this pleasant village. At the road corner, cross over the road and turn right down a lane

The village pond, Wroxton

past Glebefields Nursing Home – you will see St Peter's Church in the valley. Continue past the end of the churchyard to get back into the pleasant countryside. The path will lead you in a south westerly direction to the left of the trees.

④ Bear right between the trees and Keeper's Covert, go over the bridge across the stream and then ascend the next field towards an obelisk. Walk to the right of the obelisk and then descend to the left of the grounds of Wroxton College. A stile will allow you to walk by the fence of the old building and then bear right to walk by the park fence. A large kissing gate leads to a footpath at the side of cottages with a fence to your right. At the end of this path turn right, to arrive back in the centre of lovely Wroxton, where you will emerge near to the North Arms pub.

Wroxton Abbey was built by Sir William Pope. The building later passed to the North family, one of whose ancestors was Lord North, the Prime Minister who was responsible for losing the North American Colonies, which eventually became the United States. Royalty has been associated with Wroxton Abbey as Pope was host to King James I and King George IV slept in one of the rooms.

PLACES OF INTEREST NEARBY

Banbury Museum (5 miles S) incorporates the historic Tooley's Boatyard, being situated by the Oxford Canal. It contains a 'hands on' exhibition of the story of the canal. Telephone: 01295 259855.

North Newington
The Blinking Owl Inn

MAP: OS EXPLORER 191 (GR SP:419398)

WALK 3

DISTANCE: 2½ MILES

DIRECTIONS TO START: NORTH NEWINGTON IS 3 MILES SOUTH-WEST OF BANBURY. LEAVE BANBURY ON THE B4035, BROUGHTON ROAD. AFTER ABOUT 2 MILES TURN RIGHT TO ENTER THE VILLAGE. **PARKING:** CUSTOMERS MAY USE THE CAR PARK AT THE BLINKING OWL WHILE WALKING – PLEASE ASK FIRST.

North Newington is a peaceful country village containing a happy mixture of thatched and period cottages. Each year it is attractively decorated, with flowers lining its roads and the village green. This stroll will take you to nearby Broughton Castle and after passing to the front of the castle the route continues across attractive Oxfordshire countryside with fine views all around.

Broughton Castle was originally erected in 1306 by Sir John de Broughton as a fortified manor house. It passed into the hands of William de Wyckeham, the founder of Winchester College and New College, Oxford, who added battlements as he turned the building into a castle. The mellowed brickwork of the castle sets a fine picture reflecting in the water of the moat, which is full of colourful lilies.

The Blinking Owl Inn

This country inn was built in 1645 overlooking the original Stratford to London road. You will not be able to escape the owl, which is featured in the decoration of the inn. There are owls in the carpets and owls and other countryside animals dotted all around this lovely building, whose beamed ceilings and open log fires will appeal. You will be guaranteed a warm welcome.

Opening hours on weekdays are from 12 noon to 2 pm (noon until 3 pm at weekends) and from 6 pm to 11 pm (7-11 pm at weekends). Hook Norton beer, Marston's Pedigree, Charles Wells Bombardier (plus two guest ales) are the real ales which should be sufficient for the discerning beer drinker, while Scrumpy Jack and Dry Blackthorn will appeal to the cider drinker.

A wide selection of tasty snacks and meals cooked to order varies from a ploughman's to curries and there are specials of the day to look out for. Food is available between 12 noon and 2 pm (3 pm at weekends) and 6 pm to 9 pm during the week. At weekends evening meals are available between 7 pm and 9 pm. Sunday booking is advisable.

Children are allowed in the patio area, as are dogs, provided they are kept on a lead at all times. Telephone: 01295 730650.

The Walk

① From the Blinking Owl, turn right up the High Street in North Newington, then bear left along Park Lane. Just before reaching Park Farm, turn right past cottages to arrive in open pastureland with Park Farm and a superb dovecote to your left. Stroll southwards and exit the farmland via the farm gateway onto Banbury Road. Cross over the road and go over a stile into a cultivated field following the direction of the waymarker post (ie southwards). After walking across the field for about 200 yards, a farm gate will lead you onto a lane. Cross over the lane and continue ahead over the stile opposite, then descend the next field to its far corner to reach a farm lane. Go over the lane and over the footbridge opposite; then descend the next field to its far corner, crossing over a footbridge onto the main lane once again to arrive near to the entrance gate to Broughton Castle. Proceed along the driveway to the famous house, sparing time to enjoy the superb view of the castle and its fine lake.

② When ready, walk the clear footpath going north-west and link up with the footpath that crosses the parkland from near the lodge gate entrance. Go left up towards the main group of trees (generally to the north-west) and then stroll along the path to the right of the trees until you reach a stile in the fence ahead. Proceed over this stile and walk to the right of the field fence down to a barn.

③ At the barn, go right and stroll up the green farm track, now going generally

PLACES OF INTEREST NEARBY

Broughton Castle (3 miles SE) – the ancestral home of the Saye family for the last 600 years. The castle is open to the public 2 pm–5 pm on Wednesdays and Sundays plus bank holidays. Telephone: 01295 276070.

Broughton Castle

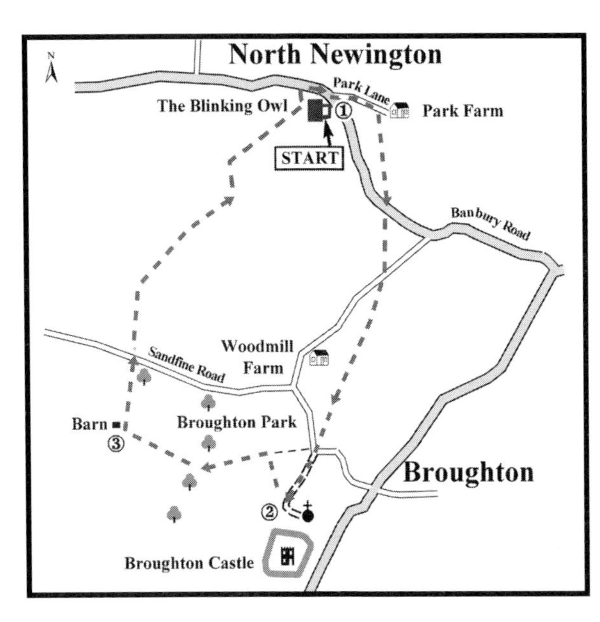

northwards. This track will lead up to Sandfine Road by the side of woodland. Cross over the road and continue ahead by the side of the next field hedge. After about 200 yards the fence bends right and soon you will go left into a large cultivated field. Bear right and diagonally cross this field to its far corner; then go left for about 100 yards before veering right to diagonally cross a final field to arrive at a track. Here, bear left and descend a lane into Main Street, North Newington, and the Blinking Owl Inn.

Adderbury
The Red Lion Hotel

MAP: OS EXPLORER 191 (GR SP:474356) | WALK 4 | **DISTANCE:** 3 MILES

DIRECTIONS TO START: ADDERBURY IS 3½ MILES SOUTH OF BANBURY ON THE A4260, OXFORD ROAD. **PARKING:** CUSTOMERS MAY USE THE CAR PARK AT THE RED LION HOTEL WHILE WALKING – PLEASE ASK FIRST.

Adderbury dates from Saxon times and today the pretty village is adorned with flowers during the summer months. Adderbury House was used to house troops during the Civil War and again in World War II. The house became the home of the 2nd Earl of Rochester. He was a lyrical and satirical poet and in 1997 a variety of events were held in Oxfordshire to mark the 350th anniversary of his birth.

In the 19th century, the Dukes of Argyll held possession of Adderbury House and a Major Larnach became famous when his horse Jeddah won the Derby. The church of St Mary the Virgin was beloved of Sir John Betjeman and is associated with New College, Oxford.

This easy walk commences with a pleasant stroll along the main road in Adderbury and then veers into attractive countryside to pass near to a white windmill which is a landmark in the area. The route then continues across pastureland before returning to the popular Red Lion Hotel.

The Red Lion Hotel

This former coaching inn is delightfully situated overlooking the village green at Adderbury. Dating back to the Civil War, the building was once a Royalist owned hostelry and inside there are old oak decorations and stone chimneys. The gardens and patio at the front of the building form a popular eating place, attracting locals and visitors alike. You will be guaranteed a warm welcome.

Opening hours are from 11 am to 11 pm (10.30 pm on Sundays). Hook Norton beer, IPA and Abbott are the real ales, while Strongbow is on tap for the cider drinker. A large selection of wines, supplied by Waverley Vintners, is always available.

A scrumptious selection of English and Continental bar food and snacks plus an à la carte menu are available. Food is available between 12 noon and 2.30 pm and between 7 pm and 9.30 pm during the week. On Sundays food can be had between 12 noon and 9.30 pm.

Children are allowed in the patio area but dogs are not allowed. Telephone: 01295 810269.

The Walk

① From the Red Lion Hotel car park cross the busy A4260, and stroll past the village green into Adderbury. Walk the length of the main street, which arcs right past the church, and then bear right into Manor Road. At the end of Manor Road you will reach the archway to Adderbury House.

② Go right and proceed through a pair of kissing gates to arrive in open farmland. After going over a footbridge and a stile, walk along the good, wide footpath going generally north-west – to your right there is a typical Oxfordshire view over cultivated land. After about ½ mile of pleasant walking you will reach a junction of paths/tracks. Continue ahead along the footpath towards trees, still maintaining your north-westerly direction, for about 500 yards up to a farm lane.

PLACES OF INTEREST NEARBY

Deddington Castle (2½ miles S) comprises extensive earthworks and the remains of the 12th-century castle. Entry is free and there is an adjacent recreational area.

③ Go right (east) along the lane and you will pass by a small white windmill and then the impressive farm complex at Bloxham Grove. Continue past the farm buildings along a good, wide, green farm track that arcs gently left and ahead you will see the edge of Banbury town. After passing through some trees you will reach Sorbrook Mill. Proceed over the bridge crossing the Sor Brook.

④ After about 150 yards, turn right past a small lake and through a hand-gate into pastureland. Walk by the left-hand field hedge and continue by going through a farm gate and over a footbridge onto a footpath that then arcs right for your return stroll back to Adderbury. Initially this path ascends gently and then continues to the right of the field hedge. As you progress you will see the village of Twyford to your left and then the path descends and you will pass to the left of Windmill Hill Farm. With the church in Adderbury visible on the skyline, aim for a

The path up from Sorbrook Mill

stile in the far left field corner and then continue to the left of the field hedge with the village coming into view. Where the path divides, bear right and you will soon arrive in Meadow View as you proceed to the centre of the village.

⑤ At the High Street go left and walk past the village green to arrive back at the Red Lion Hotel.

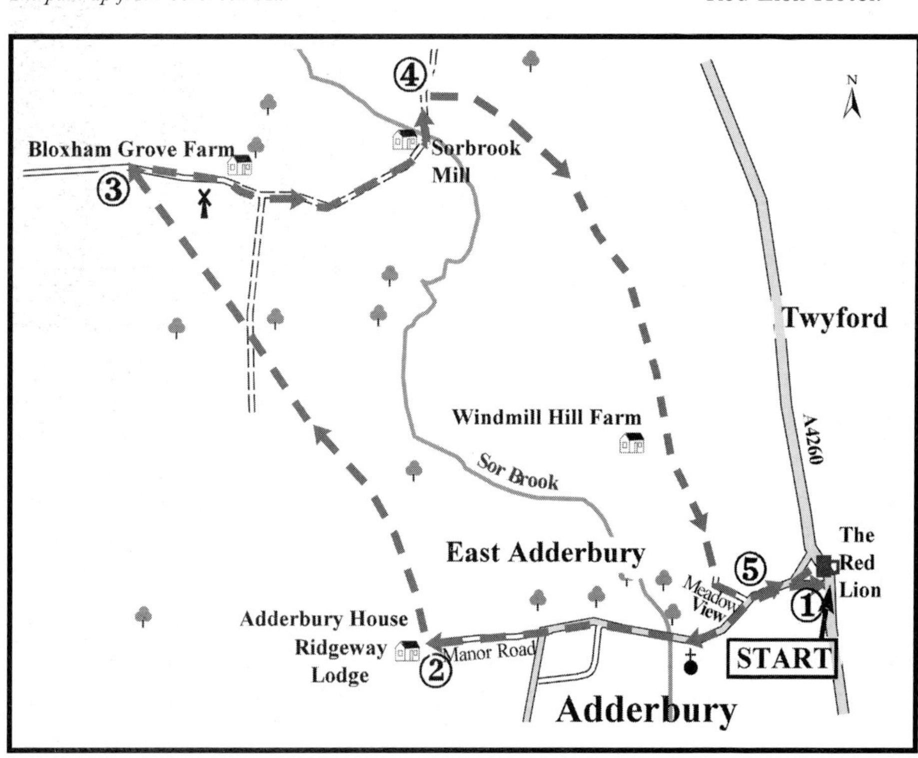

Hook Norton
The Sun Inn

MAP: OS EXPLORER 191 (GR SP:354331) — WALK 5 — **DISTANCE:** 3 MILES

DIRECTIONS TO START: HOOK NORTON IS 6 MILES NORTH-EAST OF CHIPPING NORTON. LEAVE CHIPPING NORTON ON THE A44. AT THE ROAD ISLAND CONTINUE NORTH-EAST ALONG THE A361 FOR 300 YARDS THEN BEAR LEFT TOWARDS HOOK NORTON. AT SCOTLAND END, GO RIGHT TO ARRIVE IN HOOK NORTON. **PARKING:** CUSTOMERS MAY USE THE CAR PARK AT THE SUN INN WHILE WALKING – PLEASE ASK FIRST.

Hook Norton is situated amid stunning countryside on the edge of the Cotswold Hills. It is a beautiful small town of brown stone houses and terraces. The houses spill down the hillside and are crowned by St Peter's Church, whose Norman tower tends to dominate the centre of the town. Once upon a time there was an 80 ft high viaduct that passed by the side of the town but this disappeared with the Beeching axe.

Hook Norton is famous for its local real ale, which is still made in the town. The independent concern is housed in an amazing Victorian building.

This easy stroll goes along the main street and then progresses into open countryside. The return route is along a good farm track, and there is an unusual view of the stone pillars which once carried the railway before you reach Hook Norton for your refreshments.

The Sun Inn

The Sun Inn is situated in the High Street, almost opposite St Peter's church. It has had an association with the famous Hook Norton Brewery for many years. There is a patio garden at the rear of the building or one can enjoy a quiet drink and meal in the lounge. You will enjoy seeing the ashtray that depicts the fantastic Hook Norton Brewery building.

The inn is open at lunchtime every weekday from 11.30 am to 2.30 pm (12 noon to 3 pm on Saturday and Sunday) and each evening of the week from 6 pm to 11 pm. Hook Norton Ale dominates, while Strongbow is on tap for the cider drinker. A large selection of wines is always available.

A selection of delicious bar snacks is available and an à la carte restaurant will serve home cooked fresh food to order. Food is available between 12 noon and 2 pm and between 7 pm and 9.15 pm during the week. On Sundays lunch is between 12 noon and 3 pm and evening meals can be taken between 7 pm and 10 pm.

Children and dogs are not allowed in the inn. Telephone: 01608 737570.

The Walk

① From the car park at the Sun Inn turn right along the High Street of Hook Norton and into Down End. The road arcs right as you descend Down End, passing some lovely thatched cottages, to arrive in Park Hill by a small triangular road island. Continue to the right along Park End road for about 20 yards.

② Go left up a signed footpath and ascend into trees. The path leads to a stile and here bear left to walk the fenced footpath above the trees as you progress around the north edge of the field to arrive in trees once again near to the stone pillars of the dismantled railway line. Now bear left again to join the main path through the trees and you will emerge into the open once more to walk a clear fenced footpath that hugs the field edge above the trees. Walk this good path for the next 900 yards. A gate leads into pastureland and you continue south-east to reach a footbridge over a stream.

③ Here, go left over the footbridge and follow the waymarked footpath though a small copse to arrive in the farmyard of Manor Farm. Proceed between two Dutch barns and into pastureland beyond the farm complex. Go left over a pair of stiles over the farm track and then bear right across the field.

④ Go sharp right and proceed over the farm track and descend to a hedge by a small stream. Bear right to reach a footbridge over the stream and then go left over the bridge onto a good footpath that continues in a generally westerly direction – to your left you will see a large pond where youngsters may be fishing. Continue by ascending the path and after about 300 yards bear slightly right to join a

PLACES OF INTEREST NEARBY

The Hook Norton Brewery is situated in the village of Hook Norton and its visitor centre is open daily from Monday to Friday, when guided tours are offered by prior arrangement. Telephone: 01608 730384.

Hook Norton Brewery

good track coming in from the left. This is fine walking, with Grounds Farm clearly visible over the dip to your left. You will pass through a pair of farm gates to reach a stone track that leads to the corner of Park Road in the village of Hook Norton. This passes between more of the stone pillars of the dismantled railway and you will enjoy a good view of the bridge structure. Walk between the cottages of the village to reach a road called Bell Hill.

⑤ Go right for about 25 yards, then cross the road into Middle Hill, bearing right and ascending the road back to the main street in the village. Go left to reach the Sun Inn.

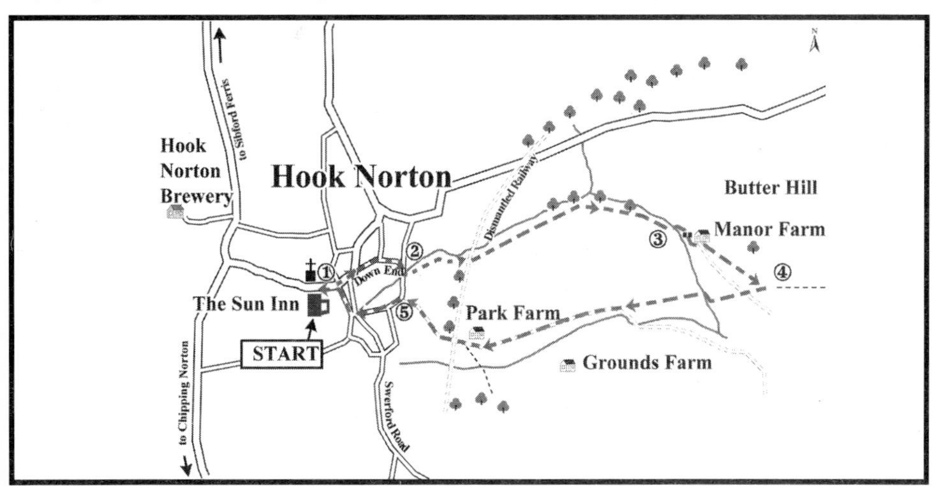

Great Tew
The Falkland Arms

MAP: OS EXPLORER 191 (GR SP:395293) | WALK 6 | **DISTANCE:** $3\frac{3}{4}$ MILES

DIRECTIONS TO START: GREAT TEW IS SITUATED 6 MILES NORTH-EAST OF CHIPPING CAMPDEN. LEAVE CHIPPING CAMPDEN ON THE A361, BANBURY ROAD. IN ABOUT 5 MILES, TURN RIGHT ONTO THE B4022, WHICH LEADS INTO THE VILLAGE CENTRE. **PARKING:** THERE IS FREE PARKING IN THE LARGE VILLAGE CAR PARK AS YOU ARRIVE IN THE VILLAGE.

Great Tew is a most beautiful village set on the edge of the Cotswolds – a village where one steps back in time. So many attractive thatched cottages line the roads, with lovely trees planted to the design of Loudon. The history of Great Tew is very much linked to Lucius Carey, 2nd Viscount Falkland (1610-1643), who was Lord of the Manor around the time of the Civil War. He, like so many after him, enjoyed walking in this beautiful part of Oxfordshire. Sadly he lost his life in the Civil War. He rode his horse directly into a hail of musket fire in battle. The village pub is named after the great man.

Great Tew is one of a few villages that have retained their own school and it remains a peaceful and picturesque place to visit.

From the car park the stroll proceeds along a lane of thatched cottages and then progresses on good farm tracks into open countryside before passing by Great Tew Park on the return route to the village.

The Falkland Arms

This award winning Cotswold village inn is a regular haunt of local walkers and you are guaranteed a warm welcome. It dates back to the 16th century, when it was originally called the Horse and Groom, and is set at the end of a row of thatched properties. It is a treat to sit out in the front garden and enjoy the unique atmosphere of the Cotswolds. In winter one can sit by the inglenook fireplace and admire a fantastic collection of mugs and jugs that hang from the ceiling and a selection of clay pipes and snuff that are on sale.

During the week, opening hours are from 11.30 am to 2.30 pm (12 noon to 3 pm on Saturday and Sunday) and from 6 pm to 11 pm (7 pm to 10.30 pm on Sundays). Wadworth's 6X, Old Timer and Henley's IPA are the real ales, although there are always guest ales available – seven real ales that vary from week to week. The pub has been awarded a Cask Marque. Inch's Harvest Dry is the cider on tap and a large selection of wines and whiskies is available.

Food is offered on a first-come-first-served basis between 12 noon and 2 pm and from 7 pm to 8 pm every day of the week. A traditional country bar menu is offered, hand raised pork pies and beef and ale pie being two of the favourites with locals and visitors alike.

There is a garden to enjoy, with children allowed in the lounge and garden only. Dogs are allowed but must be kept under control and on leads at all times. Walkers who are customers may use the car park. Telephone: 01608 683 653. Website: www.falklandarms.org.uk. E-mail: sjcourage@btconnect.com

The Walk

① From the village car park, go left into the centre of the village and go left again at the thatched post office to walk past several most beautiful thatched cottages as you descend a delightful lane. After passing by Bee Bole Cottage, the lane bends left to pass by Lower Park Farm and to reach a junction of tracks by Cow Hill. Go right, continuing along the track for about 700 yards – to your left is the lovely hill of parkland where rhododendrons add real colour in the spring.

② Now, go right and walk a farm track known as Groveash Lane for about 1½ miles – an easy stretch of walking with pleasing views over delightful Oxfordshire countryside.

PLACES OF INTEREST NEARBY

The Hook Norton Brewery (4 miles NW) is situated in the village of Hook Norton and its visitor centre is open daily from Monday to Friday, when guided tours are offered by prior arrangement. Telephone: 01608 730384.

Broughton Castle (8 miles N) – the ancestral home of the Saye family for the last 600 years. The castle is open to the public 2 pm–5 pm on Wednesdays and Sundays plus bank holidays. Telephone: 01295 276070.

③ At a junction of paths, go right and walk a footpath over cultivated land, proceeding in a generally southerly direction. Cross over the footbridge at the field corner and continue to a gap in the next field hedge, where you go left through a farm gate and proceed to a lane.

The delightful thatched post office in Great Tew

④ Do not go onto the lane but turn around and now walk the footpath that runs almost parallel with the one you arrived on, aiming for a stile set about 100 yards from the field gate you passed through. Go over this stile and continue in a generally south-westerly direction over open fields for about $1^1/_4$ miles.

⑤ At the field corner, bear right and walk the clear headland path to the right of a stone wall. This is easy walking with pleasing views to your right and with Great Tew Park over the wall to your left. All too soon you will arrive in Great Tew by the side of the Falkland Arms inn. Go right and then left to return to the car park.

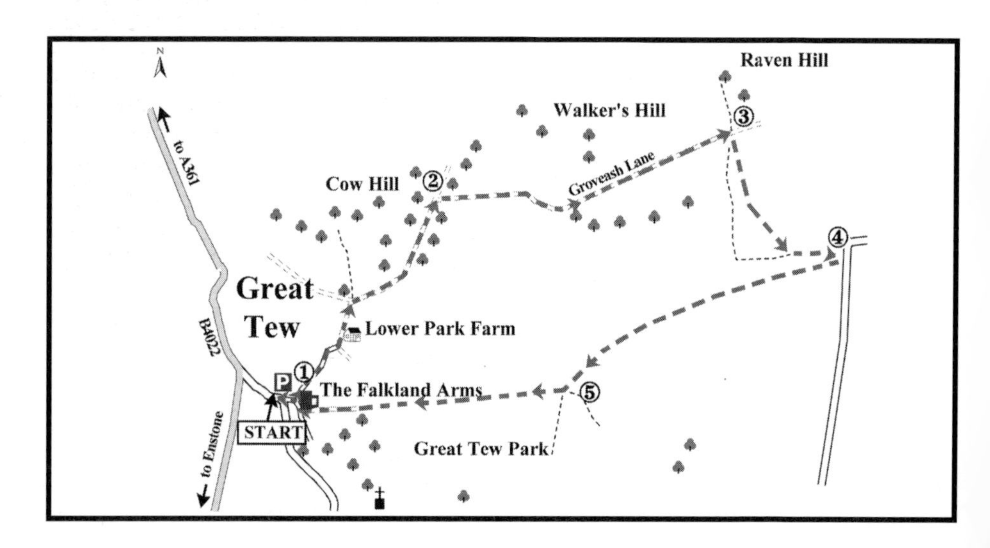

Fringford
The Butchers Arms

MAP: OS EXPLORER 191 (GR SP:605285)

WALK 7

DISTANCE: 3 MILES

DIRECTIONS TO START: FRINGFORD IS 5 MILES NORTH OF BICESTER. APPROACH THE VILLAGE FROM THE A4421. THE BUTCHERS ARMS IS AT THE END OF THE MAIN STREET NEAR TO THE CRICKET PITCH. **PARKING:** CUSTOMERS MAY USE THE CAR PARK AT THE BUTCHERS ARMS WHILE WALKING – PLEASE ASK FIRST.

The ancient village of Fringford has been inhabited for much of the last 2,000 years. The name is derived from a Saxon tribe/group and is believed to mean 'ford of the people of Fera'. The church of St Michael and All Angels dates from the early 12th century.

In the 19th century the village was associated with Flora Thompson of *Lark Rise to Candleford* fame. She grew up in neighbouring Juniper Hill and was educated at nearby Cottisford before she moved to live in Candleford Green in Fringford.

From the Butchers Arms you will stroll past the cricket pitch into open countryside. The village boasts an enthusiastic cricket club that celebrated its centenary in 2001. The route takes you over cultivated fields and you pass by the very attractive buildings of Willaston Farm before starting the return journey. There are fine views to enjoy as you reach the road outside Fringford. After strolling over a large field you will arrive in the village and pass through the churchyard en route back to the pub.

The Butchers Arms

The Butchers Arms is a delightful 18th century pub set next to the cricket ground in the attractive village of Fringford. The pub is the 'local' for the cricket team and has an interesting display of cricketing memorabilia, which includes a photograph of the famous W.G. Grace, a set of old cricket stumps, an old ball and wicket-keeping gloves. The pub is popular with local people and can be busy on match days.

Opening hours are from 12 noon to 11 pm throughout the week, including Saturdays and Sundays. Broadside, Cumberland and Pedigree are the three real ales on offer, while Strongbow is available for the cider drinker. Chardonnay is the wine.

Food is available between 11 am and 3 pm during the week and from 12 noon to 3 pm at weekends. Traditional English food is offered, including seafood and steaks; also curries.

Children are allowed in the pub, as are dogs, provided that they are kept under strict control at all times. Telephone: 01869 277363.

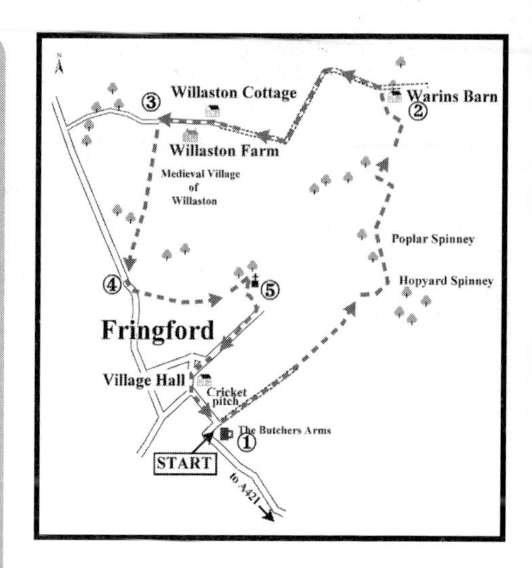

The Walk

① Exit the pub car park and stroll along the footpath/track to the left of the Butchers Arms and to the right of the village cricket pitch. Maintain a north-easterly direction for the next $^1/_2$ mile. Initially the path will be hedged but then opens out and soon you will reach a stile. Go over the stile and turn right over a footbridge and further stile into the edge of Poplar Spinney. Bear left at the spinney and proceed north-west to the field corner, then bear right and follow the field edge up the side of the next field.

② Now go left and walk the clear footpath over the corner of the field towards Warins Barn. Bear left past the old, dilapidated building onto a good farm track. Walk this track for the next $^1/_2$ mile. The track zigzags and then straightens out until you ascend a bank, towards Willaston Farm. After passing by Willaston Cottage, proceed past the buildings of the main farm onto the farm drive.

③ About 30 yards beyond the main buildings, go left and walk the footpath to the right of the field hedge, going generally south, passing by the site of the medieval village of Willaston. Proceed over the stile in the field corner by trees and continue ahead, descending to a hand-gate onto a road.

④ Go left along the road over Fringford Bridge and then go left again over a stile and ascend the hill to the village of

Making friends near Willaston Cottage

Fringford. A pair of kissing gates takes you into the village. Go left down Rectory Lane and then continue up the clear footpath that leads past the vicarage and allows access into the churchyard of St Michael and All Angels church.

⑤ Exit the churchyard through the lychgate and turn right up Church Street into the village. Stroll past a number of attractive thatched cottages (Lilac, Beagle and Folly being but three of these). The road arcs left as you pass by the large village green with the village hall on the left; you then bear left to walk along the main street back to the pub car park.

PLACES OF INTEREST NEARBY

Bicester Outlet Village (5 miles S) is an international Outlet Shopping Village where you can find some 75 famous British and international brands at reduced prices. Telephone: 01869 323200.

Claydon House, Buckinghamshire (10 miles W) – a superb National Trust house that is famous for its remarkable 18th-century rococo and chinoiserie decoration. Telephone: 01296 730349.

Chipping Norton
The Chequers

MAP: OS EXPLORER 191 (GR SP:313270) | **WALK 8** | **DISTANCE:** $2\frac{1}{2}$ MILES

DIRECTIONS TO START: CHIPPING NORTON IS SITUATED 13 MILES SOUTH-WEST OF BANBURY AND 22 MILES NORTH-WEST OF OXFORD. LEAVE OXFORD ON THE A44 AND AT THE ROAD ISLAND JUNCTION WITH THE A3400 BEAR LEFT TO REMAIN ON THE A44, WHICH GOES THROUGH THE MIDDLE OF THE TOWN. **PARKING:** PARK IN THE PAY AND DISPLAY CAR PARK AT THE REAR OF REGENT COURT OFF NEW STREET.

Picturesque Chipping Norton is an ancient hilltop market town set on the edge of the beautiful Cotswolds. After the Romans left, the Normans built a church and a castle. The church of St Mary the Virgin remains but the castle has long since been reduced to a mere mound. The church is a fine example of a 'wool church', being enlarged by the local merchants who became rich on the profits of the Cotswold wool trade. In Victorian times William Bliss built a tweed mill to replace an earlier mill that burned down in 1872. The spectacular Bliss Mill was closed in 1980 and has been converted for local government use.

This stroll passes through the old part of the town, past some lovely almshouses and St Mary's parish church on the way into neighbouring Over Norton. The gentle route continues along good farm tracks for a fine view over Chipping Norton that embraces the impressive Bliss Mill.

The Chequers

This award-winning 16th-century pub has timber beams and log fires to warm the visitor in winter. It is a Fuller's 'Pub of the Year' and proudly displays the Cask Marque for quality, not to mention the CAMRA awards.

Opening hours are from 12 noon to 11 pm throughout the week, including Saturdays and Sundays. Chiswick Bitter, London Pride and Fuller's Seasonal Ales provide the real ales for the enthusiast, while Strongbow cider is on tap for the cider drinker. There is a large selection of country and other wines available.

Traditional English fresh food is prepared on the premises and attracts locals and visitors alike. From Monday to Saturday this is available between 12 noon and 2.30 pm and 6 pm to 9.30 pm, while on Sunday food is served between 12 noon and 5 pm.

The Chequers is a friendly place with a pleasing atmosphere. Children and dogs are not allowed on the premises. Telephone: 01608 644717. Website: www.chequers-pub.co.uk E-mail: enquiries@chequers-pub.co.uk

The Walk

① From the car park proceed towards New Street but turn right up Hill Lawn Court to emerge in West Street opposite the impressive town hall. Cross over the busy road with care and continue left along Main Street above Market Square. The street tapers down (near its end); cross over the road and descend left past the Tourist Information Centre to reach the Chequers. Continue down Church Street and this will bring you to the Church of St Mary the Virgin.

② Go right along the tarmac footpath past the church and continue along a hedged footpath signed 'Over Norton ¾'. This pleasant footpath will take you along the back of private houses, from where there is a pleasing view to your left over a small valley. Eventually you will arrive on the B4026. Cross over the road and walk the pavement opposite up into the village of Over Norton.

③ Where the B4026 bends sharp right, cross over the road and go left along a wide farm drive/track signed 'RIGHT OF WAY SALFORD 1¾'. Walk this good track for about a mile, passing by Cleeves Farm complex. The track arcs gently right and you will be able to enjoy fine views. To your left the view overlooks Chipping Norton with the tall chimney of Bliss Mill visible on the skyline, while to your right the Cotswold Hills will be clearly evident.

④ Where the track bends right to

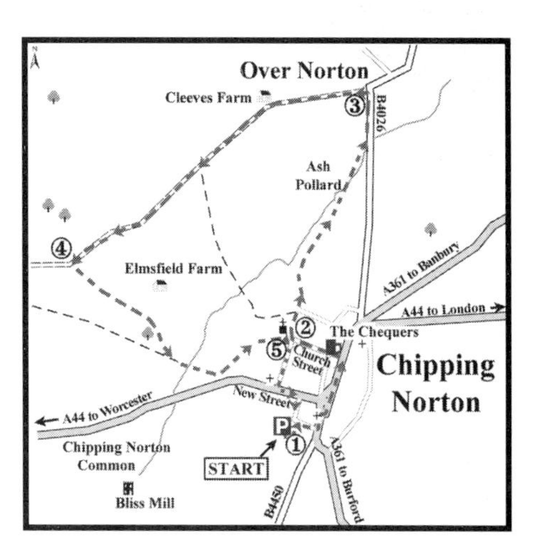

Colourful cottage in Chipping Norton

continue to Salford, go left through a fence gap and proceed to the right of the field hedge. After reaching the brow of the hill, descend over a couple of driveways to a footbridge. Ascend the hill opposite and after entering the playing field area bear left and you will be able to exit the playing field area via a kissing gate, aiming generally towards the church tower. Bear right past Mount House and enter the churchyard, where snowdrops in the spring carpet the ground. Ascend to the right of the church building.

⑤ Do not go up Church Street but go right to arrive in Diston's Lane and to reach New Street. Go left and then right to return to the car park.

PLACES OF INTEREST NEARBY

The Rollright Stones (3 miles N) are the third (behind Stonehenge and Avebury) most important Bronze Age monolithic circles in the UK. There are three sets of stones to see – King's Men, Whispering Knights and King's Stone.

Chastleton House (5½ miles W) is a fine Jacobean house owned by the National Trust. Telephone: 01494 755585.

Tackley
The Gardiner Arms

MAP: OS EXPLORER 180/191 (GR SP:478206)

WALK 9

DISTANCE: 3 MILES

DIRECTIONS TO START: TACKLEY IS 12 MILES NORTH OF OXFORD. APPROACH THE VILLAGE FROM THE A4260, BANBURY ROAD. THE GARDINER ARMS IS ON THE RIGHT JUST PAST THE VILLAGE GREEN. **PARKING:** CUSTOMERS MAY USE THE CAR PARK AT THE GARDINER ARMS WHILE WALKING – PLEASE ASK FIRST.

This short stroll meanders through the peaceful and unpretentious village of Tackley, set in beautiful countryside near to the River Cherwell. In Nethercott Road, you will pass by one of the original pubs in the village, the former Kings Head, which is now a house. The route continues along a good farm track down to the Oxford Canal and then returns to pass by two fine old gateways and an imposing three-storey thatched stable with an unusual pigeon-house – all built in Elizabethan times by John Harborne.

The Oxford Canal began life during the Industrial Revolution. Later the mainline railway was built from Banbury to Oxford and with this came modern building materials, enabling a number of the former thatched cottages in Tackley to be re-roofed with slate. The church of St Nicholas sits proudly on a hill overlooking the village like a medieval stronghold and its churchyard supports a variety of wildflowers.

The Gardiner Arms

The Gardiner Arms is an attractive pub situated around the corner from the village green in Tackley. The only pub in the village, it is well patronised by local people and visitors alike.

During the week, it is open between 12 noon and 3 pm and from 6 pm to 11 pm, while on Sundays the evening hours are 7 pm to 10.30 pm. Old Speckled Hen, IPA and Abbott are the three real ales on offer, while Blackthorn Dry cider will appeal to the cider drinker. There is a good selection of wines from all over the world for you to try.

Food is available between 12 noon and 3 pm each day and in the evenings from 6 pm to 9 pm on weekdays and Saturday, but 7 pm to 9 pm on Sunday, when booking is advisable. Bar snacks and traditional pub-style dining is offered and there is a specials board.

The Gardiner Arms has a large garden/play area and children are allowed in the pub. Dogs must be kept on leads at all times and they also are allowed in the pub. Parties of walkers (please book) are welcome. Telephone: 01869 331266.

The Walk

① From the pub, turn right up the main street in Tackley passing by the village hall.

② At the road junction, turn right along Nethercott Road. You will pass by the building of the former Kings Head pub that still displays evidence of its former occupation. At the end of the road proceed over the railway crossing and bear left up a track. In about 50 yards, go right along a clear track, walking in a southerly direction. After about 400 yards of easy pleasant walking, the track continues to the right of the field hedge as it descends gently south-east to reach the Oxfordshire Way.

③ Go left along the Way and follow the waymarkers over several footbridges to arrive on the towpath of the Oxford Canal by Flights Mill. The view of this popular canal spot may be enhanced by the presence of colourful narrowboats making their way through Pigeon Lock. Retrace your steps back over the footbridges to return to the Oxfordshire Way.

④ Go left along the Oxfordshire Way track beneath the railway bridge (you may see a Virgin train!).

⑤ About 50 yards beyond the railway bridge, turn right up a footpath set to the right of a house and proceed over pastureland going generally north. At the field hedge, bear left into the trees and cross over the footbridge. Now go immediately right along a clear footpath that passes to the right of ponds that are covered with water plants. The path arcs gently left around the watery area. Ignore

PLACES OF INTEREST NEARBY

Blenheim Palace (3½ miles SW) – the magnificent home of the Duke of Marlborough. Telephone: 01993 811325.

Bladon Church (5¼ miles SW). The churchyard contains the gravestone of Sir Winston Churchill.

The Oxford Canal

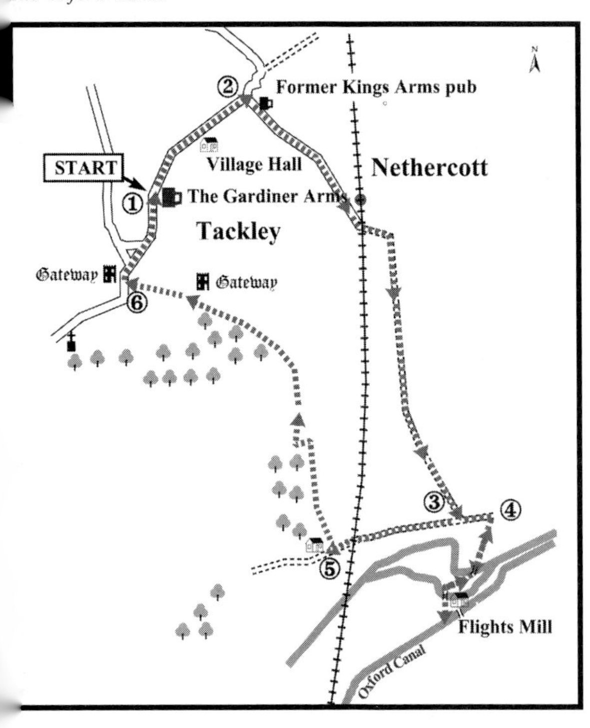

the path going right and continue left until you arrive on the road in the village of Tackley near to the gateway.

⑥ Go right along the road, past the gateway, the village green and the old manor buildings, to return to the Gardiner Arms.

Charlbury

The Bell Hotel

MAP: OS EXPLORER 180 (GR SP:356193) | WALK 10 | **DISTANCE:** 4 MILES

DIRECTIONS TO START: CHARLBURY IS 8 MILES NORTH OF WITNEY. APPROACH THE VILLAGE ON THE A4022, WITNEY ROAD. THE BELL HOTEL IS SITUATED IN CHURCH STREET. **PARKING:** CUSTOMERS MAY USE THE CAR PARK AT THE BELL HOTEL WHILE WALKING – PLEASE ASK FIRST.

Charlbury is a small, ancient Cotswold town sited on the banks of the River Evenlode and on this stroll you can enjoy some of the loveliest vistas of the Evenlode Valley. The Mercian kings owned the town in the 8th century and then, in 1094, it was given to the Norman Bishop of Lincoln, to become part of Eynsham Abbey. In 1256, Charlbury was granted a weekly charter to hold markets, although the last cattle market was held over 30 years ago, behind the Bell Hotel. The town was once well known for spinning, weaving and glove making, but most of these industries disappeared in the early 1960s.

This pleasant walk takes you along good tracks into delightful countryside. You will enjoy fine views as you stroll along part of the Oxfordshire Way, and an attractive former water mill is passed on the return route to Charlbury for refreshment.

The Bell Hotel

The Bell Hotel is one of the oldest buildings in the small, quiet town of Charlbury, carrying a date stone of 1700. It is adorned with flowers during the summer months, when the front and rear patio gardens are a delight.

It is open to non-residents from 12 noon to 2.30 pm, Tuesday to Saturday, and every evening, except Sunday, from 7 pm to 11 pm. Sunday hours are from 12 noon to 3 pm. This small friendly hotel welcomes walkers and provides a good coffee stop at the start of your stroll. Abbot and IPA real ales are offered, together with Strongbow cider in bottles. There is also a good selection of wines.

Food is available throughout the week between 12 noon and 2.30 pm, and an excellent Sunday roast is offered between 12 noon and 3 pm. From Tuesday to Saturday, food can be ordered between 7 pm and 9 pm. The menu tends to change each day to offer freshly cooked foods. There are crusty rolls with a selection of fillings, including delicious smoked salmon and cream cheese, or you can enjoy a scrumptious home-made creamy fish pie from the lunch snack menu. A separate dinner menu has many mouth-watering items.

Children and dogs (under strict control) are allowed in the hotel.

Telephone: 01608 810278. Website: www.thebellhotel.tablesir.com

The Walk

① Start the walk from the junction of

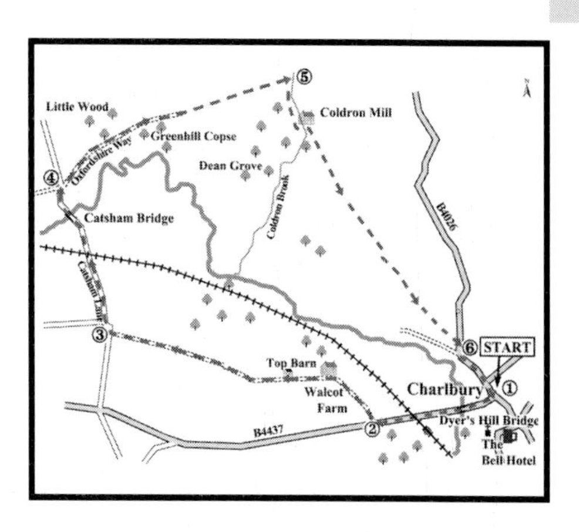

Dyer's Hill and Market Street. Proceed down the B4437 past Church Lane and continue over Dyer's Hill Bridge.

② About 550 yards after going over the railway bridge turn right along a lane towards Walcot Farm. Initially this is a tarmac road but as you progress past the farm complex the road becomes a bridleway ('to Chilson') but remains an excellent walking track. Continue along the track for about a mile. You will pass by the rather dilapidated Top Barn and there is a pleasant retrospective view over Charlbury to enjoy. The track descends to some bushes and ascends again to go through a farm gate onto Catsham Lane.

③ Go right down the quiet lane for the next 600 yards. You will cross over the railway bridge and the Catsham Bridge over the River Evenlode.

④ Turn right through a hand-gate and walk along the route of the Oxfordshire Way. After going past Little Wood and Greenhill Copse continue ahead on the bridleway – maintaining the north-easterly direction – to the north is the village of Chadlington. You will pass

Coldron Mill

through the Wychwood Project area of Dean Common, where the former sand and gravel pits are being transformed with new plantations. The bridleway descends towards the trees by Coldron Brook.

⑤ Turn right before the brook and walk the path to the right of the trees, aiming towards Dean Grove. Proceed through the kissing gate by the side of the coppice. About halfway down the side of Dean Grove, go left over a pair of footbridges to arrive in the gardens of Coldron Mill. Bear left to walk a pathway along the bottom of the gardens, then arc right. Go left over a long footbridge between stretches of water and exit into pastureland, walking generally south-eastwards. Walk the clear footpath over a long, cultivated field to reach a waymarked stile at its far end. Follow the waymarker directions as you continue south-east over several fields and through hand-gates and kissing gates until you arrive at the B4026 in Charlbury.

⑥ Walk up the right-hand side of the B4026 into the town. You will pass by Armada Cottage – built in 1587, this is the oldest building in Charlbury – and then on the other side of the road, the Quaker Meeting House by the road junction where the walk started.

PLACES OF INTEREST NEARBY

Charlbury Museum, Market Street, Charlbury – the crafts and industries of old Charlbury. Telephone: 01608 810060.

Rousham House (10 miles NE) – a beautifully furnished 17th-century house that contains a fine collection of portraits and paintings. Telephone: 01869 347110.

Woodstock

The Black Prince

MAP: OS EXPLORER 180 (GR SP:442170) | **WALK 11** | **DISTANCE:** 4 MILES

DIRECTIONS TO START: WOODSTOCK IS 10 MILES NORTH-WEST OF OXFORD. LEAVE OXFORD ON THE A44. PROCEED THROUGH THE VILLAGE OF WOODSTOCK AND THE BLACK PRINCE IS ON THE RIGHT AFTER YOU CROSS THE ROAD BRIDGE OVER THE RIVER GLYME. **PARKING:** CUSTOMERS MAY USE THE CAR PARK AT THE BLACK PRINCE WHILE WALKING – PLEASE ASK FIRST.

The village of Woodstock has retained much of its historical appearance, with many buildings dating back to the 16th, 17th and 18th centuries. The Black Prince, son of Edward III, was born here in 1331 and a deer park was established in Woodstock during the reign of Henry I. Its most famous building, Blenheim Palace, was built by Sir John Vanburgh for John Churchill, 1st Duke of Marlborough, following his victory over Louis XIV at the Battle of Blenheim.

Blenheim is the scene for this lovely stroll. The route takes you through beautiful parkland, where superb trees catch your eye and there are fine views to enjoy. There is an exceptional view of historic Blenheim Palace set in its landscape created by Capability Brown. When you arrive near to Queen Pool, take the opportunity to meander into the attractive village of Woodstock to admire the many fine old buildings.

The Black Prince

This 16th-century coaching inn is a picture of colour in the summer when beautiful flowers adorn the front of the building and the lovely patio garden that overlooks the River Glyme at its side. This popular inn has immense character with lovely timber beams and two real fires to keep you warm in winter. The heated riverside garden is a perfect place to sit and watch the world go by. The pub's car park was the scene of the murder in the first Inspector Morse novel.

From Monday to Friday opening hours are from 12 noon to 2.30 pm and from 6 pm to 11 pm. On Saturday the inn is open from 12 noon to 11 pm and on Sunday from 12 noon to 10.30 pm. Hopback Summer Lightning and Vale Brewery Best Bitter are the two regular real ales on tap together with two guest ales (all micro). Thatcher's bottled cider is available for the cider drinker and there is Hardy's Stamp wine for the wine connoisseur.

Homemade food is the order of the day and the diverse menu includes Mexican dishes, pizzas and a good range of vegetarian foods. Sunday roast is very popular and the fajitas are legendary. It is advisable to book on most days of the week – essential on Sunday.

Children are allowed in the lounge and the garden, but dogs (under strict control) are allowed only in the garden. Telephone: 01993 811530. E-mail: sarah.batkin@btinternet.com

PLACES OF INTEREST NEARBY

Blenheim Palace (½ mile S) – The magnificent home of the Duke of Marlborough. Telephone: 01993 811325.

Oxfordshire Museum (in Woodstock) – A record of Oxfordshire's heritage. Telephone: 01993 814115.

Bladon Church (2½ miles S) – The churchyard contains the gravestone of Winston Churchill.

The Walk

① From the pub car park, cross over the A44 Oxford Road and enter the Great Park at Blenheim on a public bridleway passing through a pair of timber gates. Once inside the park, turn right, stroll along the tarmac park road set above Queen Pool and proceed to the end of the pool. At the junction of park roads, go right and continue through a former quarry area, where there are some wonderful trees to admire. The road arcs left and then right – the Column of Victory is up to your left. Continue along the roadway, going north-west in a straight line towards a gate.

② Shortly before reaching the gate, bear left on a path that aims to the right of the fencing and you will find a stile on the left. Go over this stile and proceed ahead in a south-west direction passing by a fenced area of lovely horse chestnut trees and aiming for another stile set in the fence to the right. Do not go over the stile but continue ahead to the left of the fence and pass around a fenced group of superb copper beech trees to reach another stile onto the farm lane by the side of Park Farm.

③ Bear left and stroll along the farm drive that arcs gently south-east. You will pass by an area of ash trees prior to reaching a junction of tracks. Here, go right and descend between the ash tree plantation

The Column of Victory in the grounds of Blenheim Palace

and an area of conifers – there are likely to be pheasants everywhere. At the bottom of the valley proceed over the cattle grid and then, as you begin to ascend into trees, go left on a green track that curves gently left to a stile/bridlegate. Bear right to walk the clear track to the left of a large lake where you may see grebe, seagulls, coots, ducks, swans and moorhens – this is a pretty picture indeed.

④ Continue along the beech tree-lined track above the lake, enjoying a fine view of Blenheim Palace that unfolds to the right over the waters. Just after passing by a tree enclosure on the left, you will arrive by the Grand Bridge.

⑤ Retrace your steps along the track and now bear right of the tree enclosure, ascending to a junction of tracks.

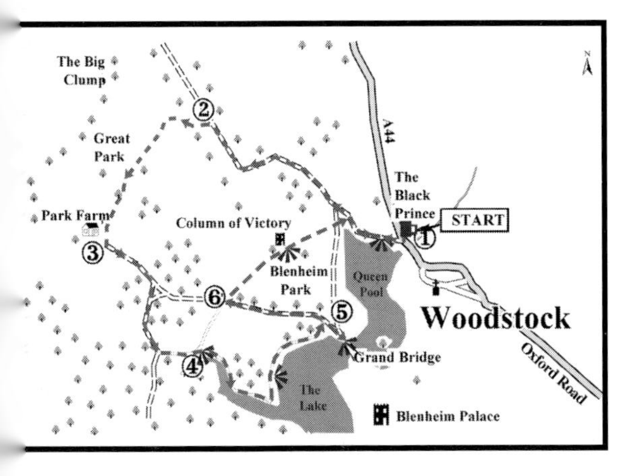

⑥ At the junction, go right and continue the ascent. The path takes you near to the superb Column of Victory for even better views over Blenheim Palace, before descending once again to arrive on the park road, near to the end of Queen Pool. Retrace your steps to the Black Prince pub.

Thrupp
The Boat Inn

MAP: OS EXPLORER 180 (GR SP:480158) **WALK 12** **DISTANCE:** 3 MILES

DIRECTIONS TO START: THRUPP IS SITUATED 8½ MILES NORTH OF OXFORD. APPROACH FROM KIDLINGTON ON THE A4260, TAKING THE LANE TO THE RIGHT INTO THRUPP TO ARRIVE AT THE BOAT INN. **PARKING:** CUSTOMERS MAY USE THE CAR PARK AT THE BOAT INN WHILE WALKING – PLEASE ASK FIRST.

Thrupp is a quiet hamlet that is situated about two miles north-east of Kidlington and set along the banks of the Oxford Canal. It comprises the Boat Inn plus a terraced row of cottages and a few other residences.

This short stroll takes you along the back of the pub and into the neighbouring village of Shipton-on-Cherwell. The path/ tracks descend to the Oxford Canal and you will enjoy pleasant waterside scenery on the towpath which is set between the Oxford Canal and the River Cherwell. You will pass close to an unusual cantilever canal bridge which lifts up to enable narrowboats to pass through and is an easy canal crossing for walkers. The route leaves the canal here and passes by some fine thatched cottages into Thrupp Community Wood, where you have a choice of paths. The permissive path is probably the most attractive because it proceeds along the banks of the River Cherwell before crossing over the main railway line to return to the canal via Sparrowgap Bridge.

The Boat Inn

Situated next to the Oxford Canal, the Boat Inn is an unpretentious Morrells pub that is popular with locals and visitors alike. There is a good folk music night on the second and fourth Sundays of each month and an occasional theatre. At the rear of the building is a large, attractive garden.

Opening hours are from 12 noon to 11 pm Monday to Saturday and from 12 noon to 10.30 pm on Sunday. Several real ales are always on tap, as is Strongbow for the cider drinker. A good selection of wines is on offer.

On Monday to Saturday food is available from 12 noon to 3 pm and 6 pm to 9 pm and on Sunday between 12 noon and 6 pm. A wide selection of home-made food with fresh vegetables is offered including steaks and light snacks. There is a daily specials board and its offerings are particularly popular.

Children and dogs are allowed in the garden but dogs are not allowed in the pub. Telephone: 01865 374279.

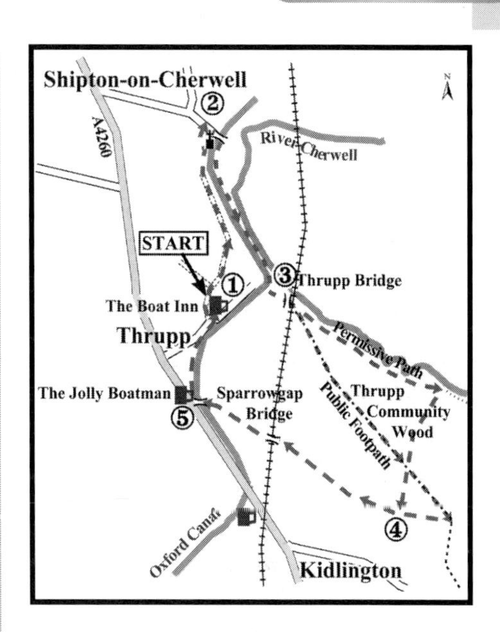

The Walk

① Start the stroll by walking along the waymarked track to the left of the Boat Inn. This track leads past cottages and through a kissing-gate, then you walk to the left of the field fence. Continue past a plantation of trees, with the Oxford Canal through the trees to the right. At the field end turn right over a stile and descend to a footpath by the side of the canal. Walk this footpath to the left of Holy Cross church in Shipton-on-Cherwell and continue through the churchyard to reach the road in the middle of the village.

② Go right and descend to the Oxford Canal, cross over the bridge and then turn right along the canal towpath. This lovely stretch of towpath will take you past a number of moored narrowboats until you arrive at Thrupp Bridge – a superb bridge that is easily raised on a fulcrum.

③ Do not cross over the bridge but go left past some thatched cottages and then walk beneath the railway bridge to a kissing-gate into Thrupp Community Wood. Here you have a choice:

(*a*) To walk the public footpath, bear right by the kissing-gate and proceed across open land for about a mile. You will go over a field stile and arrive at a junction of paths. Here, go sharp right (west) and walk a clear footpath that runs parallel with private residences in The Moors, Kidlington. At the end of the field proceed through the hedge gap into the next field.

The towpath of the Oxford Canal

(*b*) To walk the permissive path through the Community Wood, proceed ahead from the kissing-gate and walk along the banks of the River Cherwell through a plantation of deciduous trees. After walking along this path for about ½ mile, turn right (south) along a well-walked path to the left of a field hedge. The path soon ascends and you will pass by the field stile on the 'public path' route. Just over the brow of the hill go right at a field gap and join a good footpath coming in from the left; turn right along this path into the next field.

④ As you progress over this field the path arcs right (north-west) over a cultivated field and then descends to a footbridge over the mainline railway. Go over this footbridge and continue ahead to reach and cross Sparrowgap Bridge over the Oxford Canal.

⑤ Go left and descend to the canal towpath. Go left beneath the bridge and stroll past the back of the Jolly Boatman pub as you progress along the towpath, passing by a number of moored narrowboats, to return to the Boat Inn.

PLACES OF INTEREST NEARBY

Blenheim Palace (3 miles NW) – The magnificent home of the Duke of Marlborough. Telephone: 01993 811325.

Oxfordshire Museum (3 miles NW, in Woodstock) – A record of Oxfordshire's heritage. Telephone: 01993 814115.

Bladon Church (2½ miles NW) – The churchyard contains the gravestone of Winston Churchill.

Murcott
The Nut Tree

MAP: OS EXPLORER 180 (GR SP:586156) | WALK 13 | DISTANCE: 4 MILES

DIRECTIONS TO START: MURCOTT IS 12¼ MILES NORTH-EAST OF OXFORD. APPROACH THE VILLAGE ON THE A4027 AND FIND THE NUT TREE AT THE END OF THE HIGH STREET. **PARKING:** CUSTOMERS MAY USE THE CAR PARK AT THE NUT TREE WHILE WALKING – PLEASE ASK FIRST.

Murcott is one of Otmoor's 'seven towns'. Otmoor itself is a curious area of marshland that has often been described as the forgotten land. Criss-crossed by small streams, the flat moorland is liable to flooding. However, drainage systems have now been introduced and water disposal is under control. The regular flooding of properties has become a thing of the past and in springtime the streams attract a variety of butterflies and insects, and wildflowers abound along the path edges.

This stroll starts from the Nut Tree, which, like many buildings in the 'seven towns', is thatched and retains a great rustic charm. The route takes you across good paths/tracks over the marshland and through three of the 'seven towns'. While in Charlton-on-Otmoor, pay a visit to the church of St Mary to see the sumptuous rood screen with carved ribs and tracery, banded columns and linen-folded panelling.

The Nut Tree

Built in 1360, the Nut Tree is a wonderful thatched building. Its stunning appearance and character make it extremely attractive to locals and visitors alike.

Opening hours during the week are from 12 noon to 3 pm and from 6 pm to 11 pm. On Saturday the inn is open between 12 noon and 3 pm and from 6 pm to 9.30 pm, while on Sunday it opens between 12 noon and 6/7 pm. Hook Norton Best, Timothy Taylor Landlord, Brakspear's Best, West Berkshire Brewery's MR and Chubb's Lunch Time Bitter are the real ales while Thatcher's cider will appeal to the cider drinker. There is a large selection of wines to choose from.

A wide variety of excellent food is available between 12 noon and 2 pm (2.30 pm on Saturday and 3 pm on Sunday) and 6.30 pm and 9.30 pm. There is no food available on Sunday evening and only sandwiches are offered on Monday lunchtimes. All of the food is prepared on-site and there are tasty homemade sauces and desserts.

The inn has a very large garden area and this is the only part of the premises where dogs (under strict control) are allowed. Children are allowed in the conservatory and the garden. Telephone: 01865 331253. E-mail: thenuttree@aol.com

The Walk

① Exit the car park at the Nut Tree and turn right along the roadside for about 200 yards and then turn right down the driveway to Pigeon House Farm. Proceed past the farm complex on a good track.

② After 75 yards go over a stile and then turn right to a second stile to continue ahead along the left side of the field hedge, going generally north-west over a couple of fields and stiles. As you progress, the path arcs left (eastwards) and you will continue to walk to the left of the hedge and a moor stream. In about 600 yards go over a final stile and bear left onto a farm track going south-westwards. Where the track bends left go right along a hedged track to maintain your south-westerly direction. This is easy pleasant walking for some 650 yards.

③ Bear right with the track and proceed across a bridge over the New River Ray and then continue over a stream and stroll up Otmoor Lane to arrive in the attractive village of Charlton-on-Otmoor, near to the Crown Inn – the church of St Mary is opposite on the left at the junction. Continue by walking down Church Lane, opposite, and pass by a lovely thatched cottage.

④ Continue along the lane as it bends right into the Broadway and stroll past another thatched cottage. Turn right up Church Street and at the road junction bear left and walk along the verge of

PLACES OF INTEREST NEARBY

Boarstall Duck Decoy ($3\frac{1}{2}$ miles E) – A 17th-century duck decoy (National Trust) in working order. Telephone: 01844 237488.

Boarstall Tower ($3\frac{1}{2}$ miles E) – An unusual 14th-century gatehouse with gardens. Telephone: 01844 239339.

On the walk

Fencott Road to Fencott and Murcott. On the approach to Fencott there is a fine thatched house on the corner with a teddy bear on its roof, but, before you reach this building, go left and walk along Bull's Lane. The lane leads past another thatched cottage and where it bends left you pass by Ivy Farm.

⑤ In a further 100 yards, turn right to continue along Bull's Lane, which becomes a farm track, and walk along this to a junction at its end. Go left up to another junction of tracks.

⑥ Turn right and walk the waymarked field edge footpath going south-east. This good path leads into Pound Lane in Murcott, where you go right and then left to stroll along the main road in the village. After passing by the Methodist church building and a thatched cottage you will arrive back at the Nut Tree.

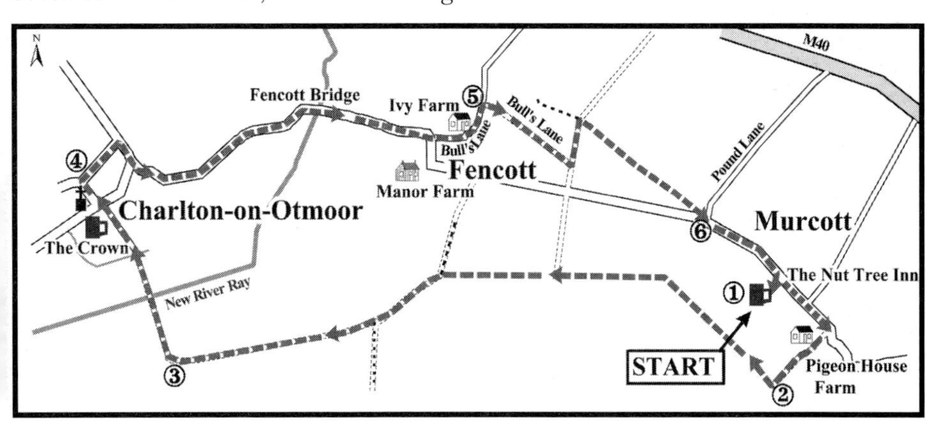

Swinbrook
The Swan Inn

MAP: OUTDOOR LEISURE 45 (GR SP:281119) | WALK 14 | **DISTANCE:** $2\frac{1}{2}$ MILES

DIRECTIONS TO START: SWINBROOK IS SITUATED 6 MILES WEST OF WITNEY AND $2\frac{1}{2}$ MILES EAST OF BURFORD. LEAVE BURFORD ON THE A40, WITNEY ROAD. IN ABOUT $1\frac{1}{2}$ MILES GO LEFT ALONG A MINOR ROAD SIGNED TO SWINBROOK. **PARKING:** CUSTOMERS MAY USE THE CAR PARK AT THE SWAN INN WHILE WALKING – PLEASE ASK FIRST.

Swinbrook is a typical Cotswold village, with attractive stone cottages lining the road for over a mile and a cricket pitch by the side of the village pub. The Windrush River meanders past the village and there is a pond scene of ducks, geese, swans, moorhens and coots. This is the paradise of the English village of old.

This pleasant stroll takes you past attractive cottages along the village lane to Paynes Farm, where you could extend your walk to see wildfowl on the pond and to enjoy the abundance of wildflowers. The return route passes through the wonderful verdant valley of Dean Bottom and you can visit the ancient church of St Oswald's before spending time in St Mary's churchyard, where the gravestones of medieval wool merchants form a fine picture.

The Swan Inn

The Swan Inn is a delightful 14th-century pub set next to a converted mill and the village cricket pitch. The landlord is an enthusiastic cricketer, and the inn is the 'local' for the cricket team – it can be busy on match days.

During the week, opening hours are from 11.30 am to 3 pm and in the evenings 6.30 pm to 11 pm. On Saturday the hours are from 12 noon to 3 pm and from 6.30 pm to 12 pm, while on Sunday the evening session finishes at 11.30 pm. Archers Village, Wadworth 6X, Morlands Speckled Hen and Green King IPA are the real ales and Weston Vintage and Stowford Press are the two ciders on tap. A wide selection of wines is on offer.

Food is available between 12 noon and 2 pm and from 7 pm to 9 pm from Monday to Friday and from 12 noon to 2.30 pm and from 7 pm to 9.30 pm at weekends (no food on Sunday evening). A comprehensive menu of food is available to cover all tastes, with special dietary needs being well met. There is always a specials menu with lots of fresh fish.

Children are allowed in the large garden at the rear of the inn but not inside the building. Dogs are allowed in the lounge and the garden. Telephone: 01993 822165.

The Walk

① From the Swan Inn, go left and stroll up the lane into the village of Swinbrook. You will soon pass by the attractive church of St Mary and should continue up the quiet lane. You will pass by a number of very attractive cottages. About $1/2$ mile from the church, look out for a stile to the left. Go over this stile and walk the clear footpath that arcs gently right and proceeds to the left of a low stone wall. Follow the path up to a gateway.

PLACES OF INTEREST NEARBY

Burford ($2^1/2$ miles W) – A most attractive Cotswold village with lots to see. Telephone: 01993 823558 (TIC).

Cotswold Wildlife Park, Burford (3 miles W) – A major family attraction in the area. Telephone: 01993 823006.

Bishop's Palace, Witney (6 miles E) – A magnificent medieval building. Telephone: 01993 775802.

② Do not go through the gate, but go left onto a nice green track that curves south-west, fairly close to Faws Grove. This is pleasant walking with nice views to enjoy as you now descend a seemingly remote area where birds sing at their best. A stone track will lead you down to a lane. Turn right and go along the lane for about 300 yards.

③ Now go left over a stile to enter a most beautiful verdant valley called Dean Bottom. With trees on either side of the valley, you can enjoy superb sheltered walking for about $1/2$ mile. As you near the bottom of the valley the view opens out once again and you will arrive near a stone wall with St Oswald church to your right. If you have time make a short visit to the church.

④ When you are ready to continue, go left and walk the clear path going generally north-east. It runs roughly parallel with the River Windrush. After negotiating a

The path passes St Oswald's church

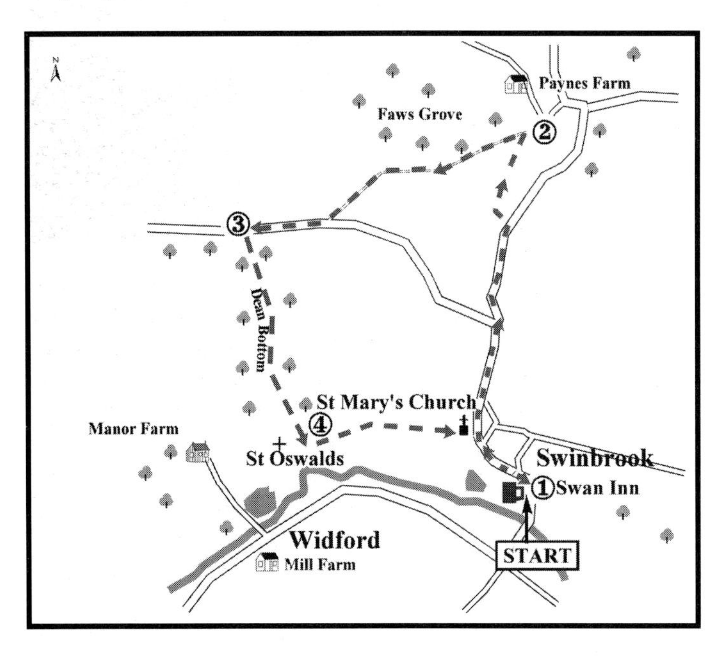

stile and then a hand-gate you will soon reach the churchyard of St Mary's. Exit the churchyard via the hand-gate onto the main road in the village and go right to return to the Swan Inn.

Beckley
The Abingdon Arms

MAP: OS EXPLORER 180 (GR SP:565112)

WALK 15

DISTANCE: 4 MILES

DIRECTIONS TO START: BECKLEY IS 6 MILES NORTH-EAST OF OXFORD. APPROACH THE VILLAGE ON THE BAYSWATER ROAD AND YOU WILL FIND THE ABINGDON ARMS IN THE HIGH STREET. **PARKING:** CUSTOMERS MAY USE THE CAR PARK AT THE ABINGDON ARMS WHILE WALKING – PLEASE ASK FIRST.

There has been a settlement at Beckley since Roman times and a Roman Road (between Alcester and Dorchester) passes through the east end of the village. Just prior to the Second World War, well paid jobs in the motor factories at Cowley attracted people away from Beckley.

After the war, however, a number of people moved out from Oxford to live in the village and fortunately they chose to retain its old-fashioned appearance by extending and enlarging many of the thatched cottages. Today the centre of the village still boasts a number of 16th- and 17th-century cottages and one can see evidence of the past in the many house names that reveal the previous occupation.

The stroll takes you over the hills, giving lovely views over the valley towards the village of Horton-cum-Studley, before you return to the old village, where you pass by thatched cottages and the fine 12th-century church of the Blessed Virgin Mary.

The Abingdon Arms

Dating back to the late 1890s, the Abingdon Arms has a large terrace at its rear overlooking Otmoor.

The pub is open all week between the hours of 11 am and 11 pm, when Brakspear and Brakspear Special are the two real ales on tap. There is a large selection of wines available for the wine connoisseur.

Food is available Monday to Saturday from 12 noon to 2.30 pm and from 7 pm to 9.30 pm in the evening (up to 10 pm on Friday and Saturday). On Sunday food is available all day from 12 noon. The pub offers good quality home-cooked food in a friendly environment and is patronised by locals and visitors alike. The specials include curries, fresh fish and a variety of foreign foods, for example, Vietnamese, Thai and French.

The garden at the rear is a true delight. Children are allowed in the bar, the lounge and the garden. Dogs must be kept on a lead when brought into the bar and/or the garden.

Telephone: 01865 351311. Website: www.woottoninns.com

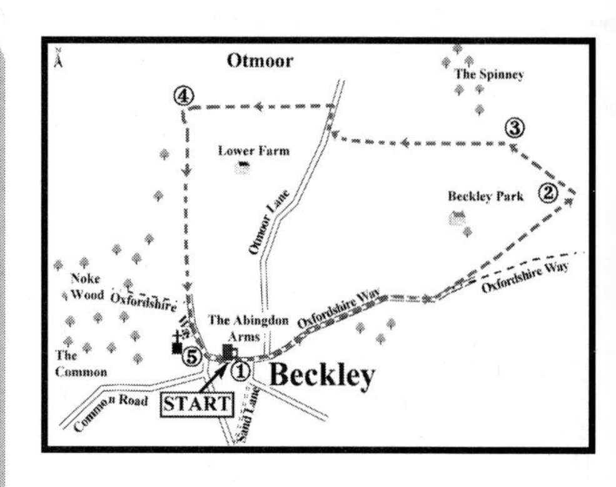

The Walk

① From the car park at the Abingdon Arms, go left and stroll past Yellow Hammer thatched cottage and ascend the track out of Beckley village, walking along the Oxfordshire Way. At the brow of the hill there is a fine view over the hills ahead. This continues as you gently descend a stone track. Follow the Way waymarkers then bear left to leave the Way on a clear footpath – maintaining your north-east direction. A couple of stiles will take you towards some trees around fish ponds and Middle Park Farm will be to your right. Exit the trees onto a farm lane and, here, go left and immediately right through a kissing-gate. Stroll along the footpath to the left of the hedge over several fields – this is Beckley Park – and to your left you will see the large house set amid the trees.

② At the end of the field go left to continue to the left of the field hedge and pass by a couple of areas where wire fencing protects new tree plantations from deer.

③ When you reach the next field corner, bear left again to continue along this good path and go over a stile – there is a military firing range on the other side of the hedge. At the next field end proceed through the hedge, over a footbridge and then walk to the right of the hedge up to a stile onto Otmoor Lane. Go right along the lane for 200 yards, then go left over a further footbridge and continue westwards by the side of a ditch, where water reeds and bulrush plants attract the wildlife. Proceed in a westerly direction over three fields and a couple of footbridges.

The route out of Beckley village

④ At the field corner, bear left (south) and ascend the field edge path to the left of the hedge. Ignore the footpath going off to the right and continue up the field to enjoy the pleasing view towards Beckley village, with the TV masts beyond. Soon you will go through the hedge and can walk a hedged footpath back into the village. As you approach Beckley, the Oxfordshire Way veers off to the right and you will arrive in Church Street. Proceed up the street past a couple of very attractive thatched houses – one is intriguingly called Bee & Church Cottage and the other is Kate Lea Cottage. Spare time to visit the super church of St Mary and then continue up the street.

PLACES OF INTEREST NEARBY

Boarstall Duck Decoy (5 miles NE) – A 17th-century duck decoy (National Trust) in working order. Telephone: 01844 237488.

Boarstall Tower (5 miles NE) – An unusual 14th-century gatehouse with gardens. Telephone: 01844 239339.

Shotover Country Park (2 miles SW) – A haven for wildlife, and preserving an ancient forest, this place of beauty is open throughout the year – there are numerous fun days out arranged in the park each year. Telephone: 01993 715830.

⑤ At the junction of roads, go left along the High Street to return to the Abingdon Arms.

Minster Lovell
The Mill and Old Swan

MAP: OS EXPLORER 180 (GR SP:318112) | **WALK 16** | **DISTANCE:** $3\frac{1}{2}$ MILES

DIRECTIONS TO START: MINSTER LOVELL IS SITUATED ABOUT 15 MILES EAST OF OXFORD. LEAVE OXFORD ON THE A40 AND AT BUSHEY GROUND TURN RIGHT, FOLLOWING THE SIGNPOSTS TO MINSTER LOVELL. **PARKING:** CUSTOMERS MAY USE THE CAR PARK AT THE MILL AND OLD SWAN WHILE WALKING – PLEASE ASK FIRST.

Minster Lovell is an ancient village set on the banks of the River Windrush. The river provided fish for food, and marshland for gamefowl and thatching reed.

The central part of the village has retained its shape for some five centuries, since, in 1431, William Lovell, the Lord of the Manor, breathed life into the village. On his return from service in France he settled in Minster Lovell and rebuilt the manor house and the church of St Kenelm – he died in 1455 and is commemorated in the fine church. Minster Lovell Hall passed to his son but changed ownership many times afterwards. Today, it is a ruin.

This lovely stroll takes you past the beautiful thatched cottages that line the main street of this delightful village. Enjoy the fine views as you stroll above the Windrush river into the nearby village of Crawley. The return route is along the river bank and you will pass by the superb ruins of Minster Lovell Hall, the church and the recreation area.

The Mill and Old Swan

Sited near to the Windrush river, The Mill and Old Swan offers a satisfying blend of Cotswold half-timbering and slate. Domesday Book records three mills in the village and it is likely that the fulling mill would have been on the site of the inn's new conference centre. The inn was added in the 15th century, and like much of the village of Minster Lovell it has changed little in appearance over the years.

At the start of the 20th century, The Mill and Old Swan was very popular with Oxford students, who, on completion of their exams, would celebrate by buying beer and singing through the night. Sir Winston Churchill was a regular visitor and Harold and Mary Wilson spent their honeymoon at this delightful hotel. The three notorious highwaymen, Tom, Dick and Harry also stopped here.

Today the hotel makes visitors very welcome throughout the week – opening hours are from 11 am to 11 pm. Hook Norton is always on tap, together with several other real ales. Food is available between 12 noon and 2.30 pm throughout the week and weekends. In the evenings, food can be ordered between 7 pm and 9 pm from Sunday to Thursday, and between 7 pm and 9.30 pm on Fridays and Saturdays. A full bar snack menu is offered together with tasty items from the restaurant menu. There is a lovely garden and children are allowed in the building. Dogs are also allowed on the premises, provided that they are always under control and on a lead at all times. Telephone: 01993 774441. Website: www.initialstyle.co.uk

The Walk

① From the Mill and Old Swan car park proceed up The Street (the main street) of Old Minster, taking time to admire the many fine old 16th/17th-century Cotswold cottages. Continue past the signed turn-off to Minster Lovell Hall and after a further 100 yards turn right onto a footpath signed 'Crawley 1'. Proceed across the pastureland, taking time to admire the ruins of Minster Lovell Hall and the attractive dovecote to your right. Initially aim for a stile in the hedge ahead and then progress by the side of the hedge/fence over several fields. After about ½ mile of very pleasant walking, you will reach a cattle enclosure and can then ascend a hedged track. Soon you will be walking a lane that leads to a T-junction of lanes. At the junction, go right along Farm Lane and you will pass in front of Rose Cottage before descending into the pretty village of Crawley, where you will pass the Lamb Inn as you reach the road junction.

② Now go right and walk the pavement – you will pass by a number of tiny

PLACES OF INTEREST NEARBY

Witney (3 miles E) is a blanket-making town with a Cotswold atmosphere. There is an unusual 17th-century Butter Cross and a tree-lined Church Green overlooking a row of 17th- and 18th-century houses. The old Blanket Hall has an unusual one-handed clock. This is a pleasant town to explore. Visitor Information Centre, telephone: 01993 775802.

The ruins of Minster Lovell Hall

residential bridges designed to allow access to the cottages by the village stream. Continue over Crawley Bridge, taking care where it narrows. Ten yards beyond the bridge, go left onto a hedged bridleway (it is signed 'Circular Walk Bridlepath – WITNEY') through pleasant pastureland for some 600 yards of delightful walking.

③ At the junction of paths, go right and ascend a footpath to arrive at Dry Lane. Cross over the lane and continue down the path opposite (signed 'Circular Walk Footpath – MINSTER LOVELL 1¼') and you will descend through trees to continue along a pleasing path by the side of the River Windrush.

④ Soon you will enter a further area of trees and will reach and cross a footbridge over the river to enjoy a very fine view of the ruins of Minster Lovell Hall, the dovecote and St Kenelm's church. The old hall is an English Heritage site and you should take the opportunity to explore the various buildings. After visiting St Kenelm's church, leave the churchyard by going over the stile in the west wall and continue along the footpath through the fields at the back of the cottages in The Street. When you reach the cricket pitch, bear right and exit the recreation area through a metal hand-gate onto the road in the village, opposite to the Mill and Old Swan.

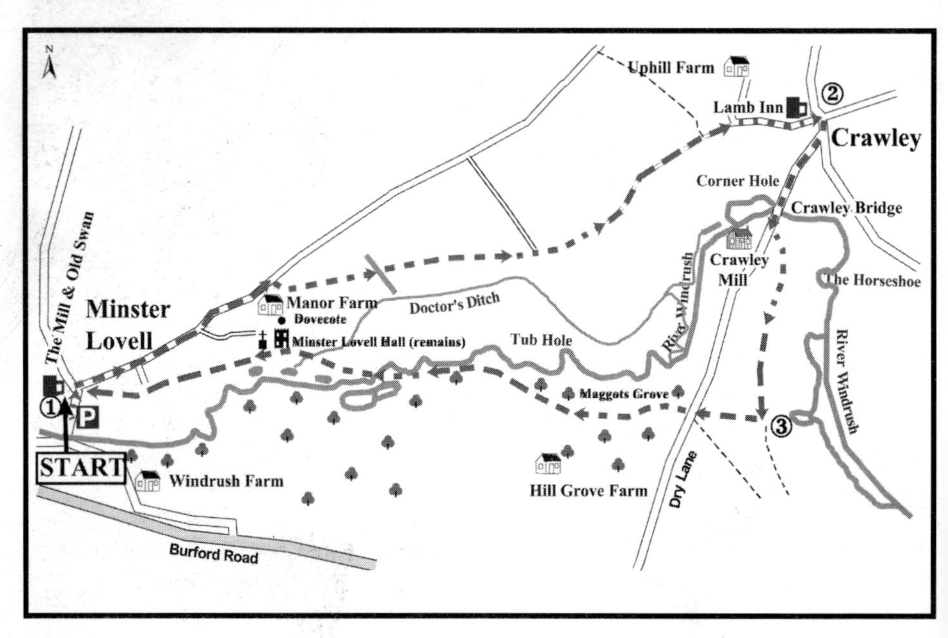

Oxford
The Crown

MAP: OS EXPLORER 180 (GR SP:512063)

WALK 17

DISTANCE: 1½ MILES

DIRECTIONS TO START: OXFORD IS 65 MILES WEST OF LONDON. THE TOURIST INFORMATION OFFICE IS IN WORCESTER STREET IN THE CITY. **PARKING:** PARK IN ONE OF THE PARK AND RIDE CAR PARKS OUTSIDE THE CITY AND TRAVEL IN ON THE BUS.

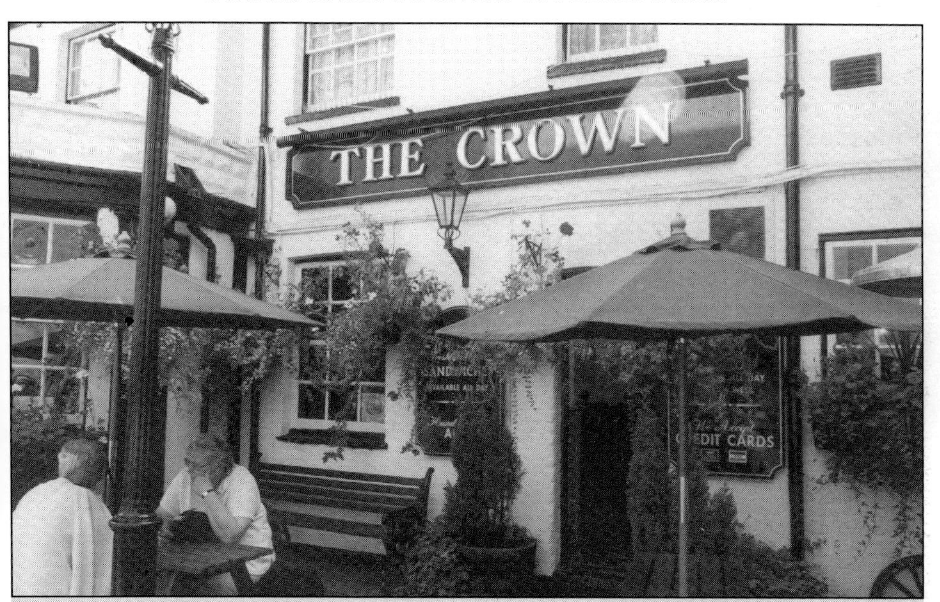

To visit Oxford is to experience history. It appears that every street is filled with beauty and the city is summed up by John Keats: 'This Oxford, I have no doubt is the finest City in the World'. The greatest collection of golden stone buildings in the world is crammed into just one square mile. There are magnificent university colleges, superb church spires and a number of impressive towers plus the wonderful dome of Radcliffe Camera – so many ancient buildings to admire and yet the city is vibrant with youthful activity as hundreds of students scurry around the streets.

This stroll takes you past many of the city's fine buildings and as the hour passes you will be treated to the sound of dozens of clock bells ringing out the time. Visit the city on a sunny summer evening and enjoy watching the punts gliding along the river and perhaps one of the apparently endless number of colourful ceremonies and sporting events that take place here.

The Crown

The Crown is situated near to Carfax Tower in the centre of Oxford. It can be found in an alley on the left as you stroll up Cornmarket Street. This attractive, lively pub dates back to 1535. It was one of the first coaching inns in Oxford and William Shakespeare is known to have stayed here. He was a great friend of the vintner, a John Davenant, and is believed to have been even friendlier towards John's wife. Shakespeare was godfather to William Davenant, who became Poet Laureate.

Opening hours are 11 am to 11 pm Monday to Saturday, and from 12 noon to 10 pm on Sundays. Various real ales are always on tap and Strongbow will please the cider drinker.

Food is served between 11 am and 8 pm during the week and between 11 am and 10 pm on Sundays. A wide menu offers snacks/light bites – jacket potatoes, hot and cold sandwiches, ploughman's – and a range of appetising main courses with a variety of tasty side orders, including pepper sauce, baby Caesar salad and Cajun onion rings. Who can resist a chocolate puddle pudding?

Children are allowed in the pub and in the patio area by the pub. Dogs are allowed on the patio, and must be kept on a lead at all times. Telephone: 01865 813961.

PLACES OF INTEREST NEARBY

Shotover Country Park (2 miles E) – A haven for wildlife, preserving an ancient forest, this place of beauty is open throughout the year – there are numerous fun days out arranged in the park each year. Telephone: 01993 715830.

Blenheim Palace (9½ miles NW) – The magnificent home of the Duke of Marlborough. Telephone: 01993 811325.

Oxfordshire Museum at Woodstock (9½ miles NW) - Oxfordshire's heritage. Telephone: 01993 814115.

The Walk

① From the Tourist Information Office walk up Worcester Street to its corner (Worcester College is here) and bear right into Beaumont Street. Proceed along Beaumont Street past the Ashmolean Museum. At the end of the street, turn right, passing Balliol College, and continue into Broad Street. Go left along Broad Street, passing to the front of Balliol College and Blackwells bookshop, and pause for a fine view of the History Museum and the Sheldonian Theatre on the corner opposite.

② Turn right down Catte Street, taking time to admire the Bridge of Sighs, modelled on the famous bridge in Venice, and visit the old Bodleian Museum Library – the library was refurbished by Thomas Bodley, a fellow of Merton College. Bear right around the fantastic Radcliffe Camera (this is part of the Bodleian Library) and continue ahead into High Street. Cross over High Street and proceed down Oriel Street opposite – Oriel College is on the left and Corpus Christi College on the right as you bear left along Merton Street. Walk the length of Merton Street, passing by the Postmasters' Hall, then arc left past the Examination Schools to arrive in High Street, opposite St Edmund Hall.

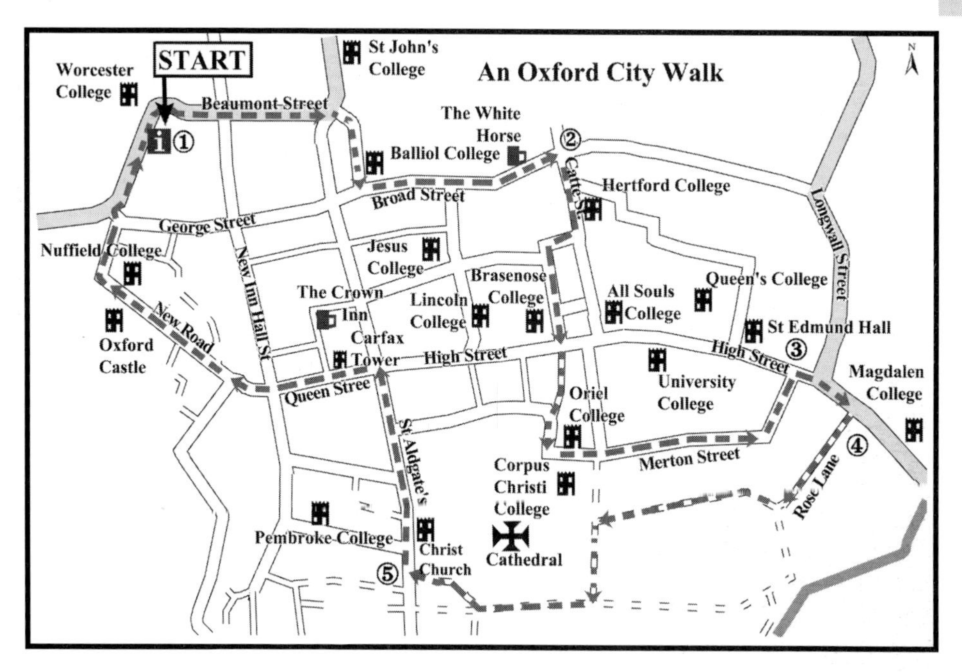

③ Turn right along the pavement of High Street for a fine view of Magdalen College and its impressive church tower.

④ Turn right into Rose Lane (with the Botanical Gardens on the left) and continue into a park area. At the junction of paths bear right and stroll along Dead Man's Walk past the back of Merton College – the oldest of the colleges. Continue along the path past the superb buildings of Christ Church College and exit onto St Aldate's.

⑤ Turn right up St Aldate's, past the front of Christ Church College, and continue up to the junction with Queen Street to see the Carfax Tower – there is a superb view from its top. The historic Crown inn is situated in an alley on the left of Cornmarket Street. From the Carfax Tower stroll along Queen Street into New Road to see Oxford Castle and proceed past Nuffield College. At the end of New Road, bear right to return to the Tourist Information Office.

Merton College

Thame
The Bird Cage Inn

MAP: OS EXPLORER 180 (GR SP:706059) | WALK 18 | **DISTANCE:** 3 MILES

DIRECTIONS TO START: THAME IS 14 MILES EAST OF OXFORD. FROM THE M40 TAKE THE A418 INTO THAME. ENTER THE TOWN FROM THE AYLESBURY ROAD AND YOU WILL FIND THE CAR PARK ON THE LEFT IN NORTH STREET. **PARKING:** PARK IN THE NORTH STREET CAR PARK IN THAME.

Thame is an ancient town. Every autumn its broad, mile-long High Street is packed with a colourful fair to coincide with the Thame Show. The High Street is lined with interesting old properties dating from the 15th century to the present day and has a picture postcard appearance. The Bird Cage Inn is a gabled and timber-framed building which is said to have been the local lock-up. There are three other old inns along the High Street. The fine town hall (1888) is very much in the centre of the street and behind this is Hampden House – formerly the Greyhound Inn – where John Hampden died after being wounded in the battle of Chalgrove in 1643.

The stroll takes you past many fine old buildings in the attractive town and you will pass through the churchyard of St Mary's. The route extends to embrace some pleasant countryside as you visit the village of Moreton before returning to the historic town centre.

The Bird Cage Inn

Originally, the bird cage was a market structure built on the lines of the stocks and whipping posts, in which lepers and thieves were imprisoned. In the reign of Edward VI the rent for this beautiful historic pub was 8 shillings per annum. French prisoners were held in the cellars during the Napoleonic wars. Situated in the High Street near to the town hall, the 13th-century black and white Bird Cage offers a fine photo opportunity, with its pair of oriel windows set in oaken frames. At the front of the building is an attractive enclosed patio and in summer months there can be no better place from which to watch the world go by.

Opening hours are from 12 noon to 11 pm, Monday to Thursday, and from 12 noon to 1 am on Friday and Saturday. Sunday hours are 12 noon to 8 pm. Bombardier, Brakspear and London Pride are the real ales on tap and there are over 30 types of wine available by the glass.

A wide selection of food is available throughout the day including a variety of delicious homemade offerings. The tapas, fresh fish, steaks and light snacks are particularly popular. There is a daily specials board which locals and visitors often select from.

Neither children nor dogs are allowed in the pub.

Telephone: 01844 260381. E-mail: birdcagepub@hotmail.com

The Walk

① Exit the car park into North Street and go left past the Two Brewers pub up towards the High Street. Turn right along Buttermarket and pass along the back of the Bird Cage Inn and the town hall (built in 1888). Turn right down Bell Lane, passing by the lovely thatched Croft Cottage, and continue to the road island at Aylesbury Road. When just round the corner into Aylesbury Road, go left through a kissing-gate into Court Close. Cross over the cricket ground, avoiding the cricket square, and proceed into St Mary's churchyard, walking along the 1887 Jubilee avenue of lime trees.

② After visiting the lovely family church, exit the churchyard at its rear into Priestend, where the prebend was erected in 1146 – today you will be able to see the 1930 gatehouse but will not be able to visit the private property. Go left and stroll up Priestend, then go left along the High Street.

③ When you have passed by Church Road (note the bandstand by Stuart House), cross over the street and walk down Brook Lane. Walk along this quiet lane past St

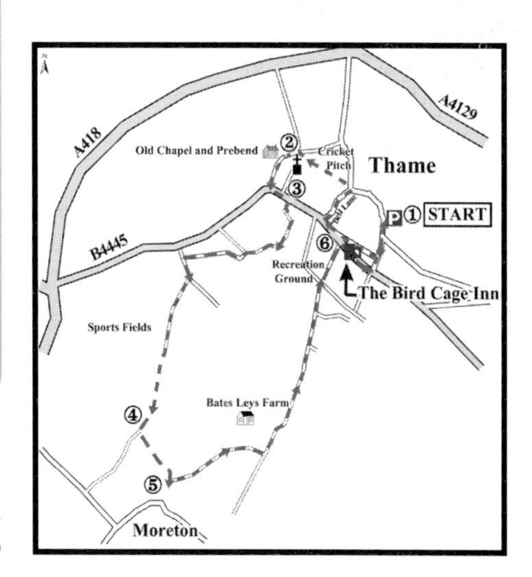

Gateway to the chapel and prebend

Joseph's Roman Catholic church, then proceed along a hedged tarmac footpath called Spring Path. This path leads over a footbridge and emerges onto Beech Road. Turn right along the road and then go left into Sycamore Drive.

④ After about 100 yards, go right along a waymarked footpath signed 'Moreton ½'. Initially the hedged path goes along the back of houses, with a school and playing fields to the right. Soon the path crosses over a disused railway and emerges through a farm gate into pasture land. Continue to the right of the field hedge. At the end of the field bear left over a stile, then go left over a footbridge into a further field. Proceed across the field aiming for a stile set to the right of a terrace of houses. Proceed past the pond onto the lane in Moreton village.

⑤ Go left up a hedged tarmac footpath set to the left of houses. After the path curves right, at a junction of paths, go left and stroll the good track past Bates Leys Farm to arrive in Moreton Lane, Thame with a recreation ground to the left. At the mini-roundabout, cross over into Lincoln Place, passing by a car park and a small residential development, to arrive in the High Street near to the town hall.

⑥ Turn right and go along the High Street to the Bird Cage Inn.

PLACES OF INTEREST NEARBY

Waddesdon Manor, Buckinghamshire (11 miles N) – The magnificent Renaissance-style château created by Baron Ferdinand de Rothschild in the 1870s. Telephone: 01296 653226.

Rycote Chapel (4 miles SW) – A fascinating English Heritage 15th-century chapel that has associations with Queen Elizabeth I and Charles I.

Stanton Harcourt

Harcourt Arms

MAP: OS EXPLORER 180 (GR SP:415057) | WALK 19 | **DISTANCE:** 2 MILES

DIRECTIONS TO START: STANTON HARCOURT IS 10½ MILES WEST OF OXFORD. AFTER BY-PASSING EYNSHAM, TAKE THE A4449 AND FOLLOW THE SIGNS TO STANTON HARCOURT. THE HARCOURT ARMS IS ON THE RIGHT IN THE VILLAGE. **PARKING:** CUSTOMERS MAY USE THE CAR PARK AT THE HARCOURT ARMS WHILE WALKING – PLEASE ASK FIRST.

The village of Stanton Harcourt is situated amid attractive meadowlands to the west of Oxford. Aerial photographs have revealed the existence of a Bronze Age settlement; three prehistoric stones (known locally as 'The Devil's Quoits') can be seen in a nearby field. The village was acquired by the Harcourt family around 1150 and has remained in their possession since then.

A central feature of the village is the Manor House, which embraces a medieval tower where Alexander Pope lived while translating Homer's *Iliad*. He left a record on a pane of glass: 'In the year 1718 Alexander Pope finished here the fifth volume of Homer'. The church of St Michael houses a collection of Harcourt monuments and tombs, including one for the standard bearer to Henry Tudor at Bosworth Field in 1485, and also Sir William Harcourt's.

This is an opportunity to stroll through a picture of feudal England. The stroll starts in the attractive village of Stanton Harcourt, then veers off into the village of Sutton, where thatched cottages line the road. On the return into Stanton Harcourt the route passes by the Manor House and the fine Pope's Tower.

Harcourt Arms

Situated opposite to Harcourt Manor and St Michael's church, the Harcourt Arms was once owned by the Harcourt family and retains a feeling of feudal England. The impressive frontage of the picturesque inn is matched by a superb interior, with an excellent rear garden, that is a treat to visit in the summer months.

The inn is open for business during the week from 11 am to 11 pm with a happy hour (Monday to Friday) from 4.30 pm to 6.30 pm. On Sundays the opening hours are 12 noon to 10.30 pm. The real ales available are London Pride, Greene King IPA, Adnam's and 6X, while Strongbow is offered to the cider drinker.

The inn is open for morning coffee at 10 am every day, and during the week lunch can be taken between 12 noon and 2.30 pm. Meals can be enjoyed between 12 noon and 10.30 pm on Sunday, when booking is advisable. There is an excellent 'bar and garden' menu with a *plat du jour*. If you have time to spare, there is an extensive à la carte menu to select from.

Children and dogs (under strict control) are allowed in the inn. Telephone: 01865 881931. E-mail: meals@harcourtarms. com

PLACES OF INTEREST NEARBY

Ashton Pottery (6½ miles W) – A chance to learn about the process of making pottery from start to finish. Telephone: 01993 852031.
Oxford Bus Museum (8 miles N) – Some 40 vehicles and other exhibits to see. Telephone: 01993 833617.

The Walk

① From the car park at the Harcourt Arms, go left and stroll through the beautiful village past a number of thatched cottages. Where the main road bends left, turn right along the waymarked tarmac footpath. Once you are clear of the residential area you will pass by the infant school and the path arcs left past the Leys play area and then continues into the village of Sutton.

② On the road in Sutton there are more thatched cottages to see to the left but you turn right and go through the pleasant village in an easterly direction. Shortly after passing by yet another thatched cottage and where the road curves gently left, turn right up the drive towards Lower Court Farm. In 50 yards, go left over a stile into pastureland and aim for a waymarked stile at the end of the field. Go over the stile and walk the path through trees to open land.

③ Go right and walk the field edge over a couple of fields and footbridges onto a clear, wide footpath over a large, cultivated field, aiming for a gap in the hedge ahead.

④ Go through the hedge gap onto Steadys Lane and turn right towards the village of Stanton Harcourt. The lane leads past a small area of woodland where there are young horse chestnut trees on the right and more mature elder trees on the left. You will pass by a farm gate and then a number of residential properties. As the lane proceeds you will pass by a number of delightful thatched cottages and then arrive at the main street in Stanton Harcourt.

The Chapel, Pope's Tower and St Michael's church

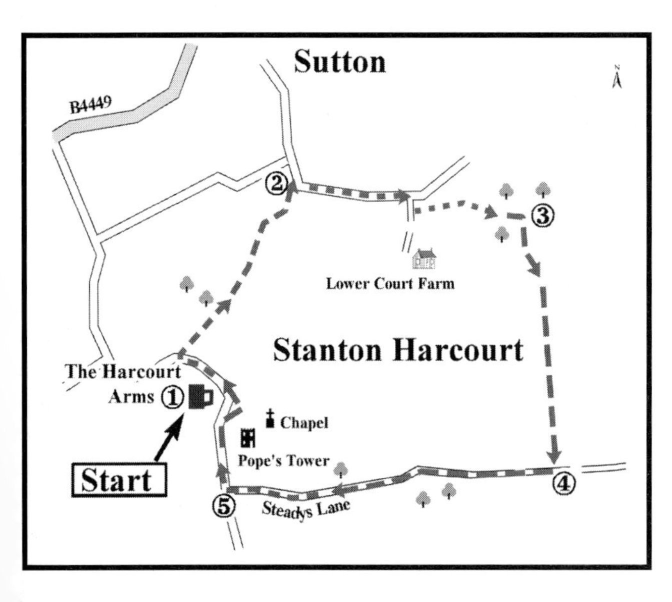

⑤ Turn right along the main street and stroll back into the centre of the village to visit the Chapel, Pope's Tower and St Michael's church on your way back to the Harcourt Arms.

Great Milton
The Bull

MAP: OS EXPLORER 180 (GR SP:630027) | **WALK 20** | **DISTANCE:** $2^3/_4$ MILES

DIRECTIONS TO START: GREAT MILTON IS SITUATED 10 MILES SOUTH-EAST OF OXFORD. APPROACH FROM EXIT 7 OF THE M40 MOTORWAY ON THE A329 – THE VILLAGE IS JUST 2 MILES SOUTH-WEST OF EXIT 7.
PARKING: CUSTOMERS MAY USE THE CAR PARK AT THE BULL INN WHILE WALKING – PLEASE ASK FIRST.

Great Milton is a fairly large, stone village set amid pleasant Oxfordshire countryside. It is said to be the home of the poet John Milton and is renowned for the fine tomb, with carved relief, of Sir Ambrose Dormer, who fought in Calais in 1347 and is buried in the church. All that remains of the Dormer mansion is a Renaissance gateway set in the wall near to the church.

Today Great Milton is probably better known for the fact that the restaurant and hotel Le Manoir aux Quat' Saisons is located on the edge of the village.

This pleasant walk starts from the beautiful thatched Bull inn and takes you through the village past the church and the Manoir hotel, then crosses the A329 onto a fine track with pleasing views. Good tracks lead into the neighbouring village of Great Haseley, where you will be able to stroll up a most delightful road. The return route goes past an old windmill that dominates the skyline before you arrive back at the Bull in Great Milton.

The Bull

The Bull is a delightful 17th-century thatched pub, which is timber-framed and has a welcoming inglenook open log fire to keep you warm in winter. It is a real picture in summer, when colourful flowers adorn its frontage.

From Monday to Saturday, opening hours are from 11.30 am to 2.30 pm and in the evenings from 6 pm to 11 pm. On Sunday the pub is open from 12 noon to 3 pm and from 7 pm to 10.30 pm. IPA and Ruddles County are the real ales on offer and Strongbow cider is available for the cider drinker. A wide selection of wines is always available.

Food is available between 12 noon and 2 pm and from 6 pm to 9 pm from Monday to Saturday and between 12 noon and 2 pm on Sundays, when booking for lunch is advisable. (No food on Sunday evening.) An extensive menu offers a range of foods from sandwiches to pasta, fish and meat. Look out for the steak on a stone as this is the local favourite. There is a specials board.

Children (under control) are allowed in the pub and in the large garden at its rear. Dogs (under strict control) are allowed in the bar and the garden. Telephone: 01844 279726.

The Walk

① Start the stroll by walking left from by the Bull, through the village of Great Milton. You will pass by some lovely old buildings including the priory, the entrance to Romeyns Court, The Great House and then, after rounding the bend, the church and Manoir aux Quat' Saisons. Continue up to the A329.

PLACES OF INTEREST NEARBY

Waterperry Gardens (4 miles N) – Eight acres of superb ornamental gardens. Telephone: 01844 339226.

Shotover Country Park (6½ miles NW) – A haven for wildlife, and preserving an ancient forest, this place of beauty is open throughout the year – there are numerous fun days out arranged in the park each year. Telephone: 01993 715830.

② Cross over the A329 with great care and proceed ahead through the metal gate opposite onto a green farm track going generally south/south-east. You will enjoy a pleasing view over Haseley Wood ahead but will soon arrive at a farm track junction.

③ Go left and stroll along the good track towards the village of Great Haseley. You will pass by a large block of farm buildings and then arrive on the Great Haseley road near to Sands Farm. Proceed ahead into the village, walking the grass verge of the quiet road. The road bends left and then right and soon you will arrive by some attractive thatched cottages. If you bear left up the lane by the cottages (Mill Lane), you will be treated to seeing a number of beautiful thatched cottages – it seems out of place to have a tiled roof. Continue along the main street of the village and you will pass by the Plough Inn and will note the lovely old post office.

④ Immediately after passing by the village school, go left up a waymarked track at the back of the school building. This track bends right and soon you will reach a junction of tracks near to the dilapidated Glebe Farm. Here, go left and walk along a wide footpath set to the right

The old windmill

of the field hedge. There is a gentle view to the left and up to your right you will be mesmerised by an old windmill (minus its sails). After walking this footpath for about $^3/_4$ mile, go left past the buildings of a small industrial estate, then right to reach the A329 once again.

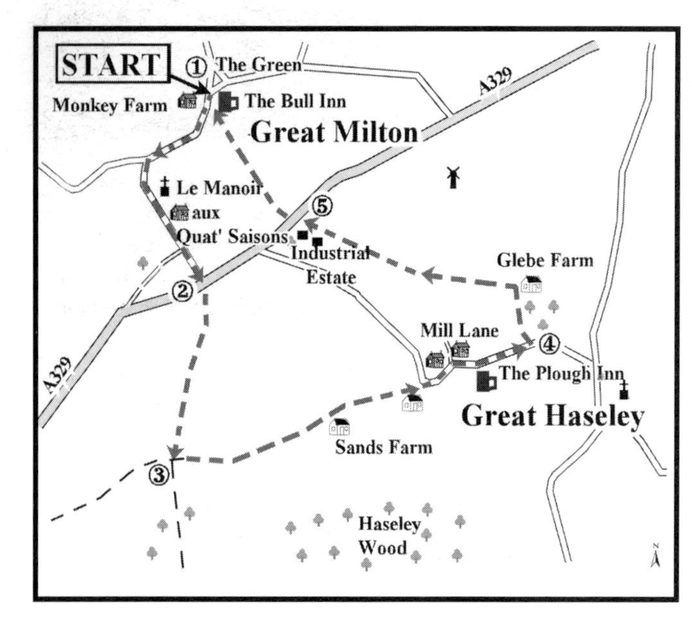

⑤ Cross over the road with care and proceed through the hand-gate opposite. The final stretch of your stroll will take you along a good footpath that eventually emerges via a track set by the side of the beautifully thatched Bull inn.

Kelmscott
The Plough

MAP: OS EXPLORER 170 (GR SP:249991) | **WALK 21** | **DISTANCE:** $1\frac{1}{2}$ MILES

DIRECTIONS TO START: KELMSCOTT IS 3 MILES EAST OF LECHLADE. FROM LECHLADE TAKE THE A417. BY THE TROUT INN, GO LEFT AND FOLLOW THE SIGNS TO KELMSCOTT. **PARKING:** CUSTOMERS MAY USE THE CAR PARK AT THE PLOUGH WHILE WALKING – PLEASE ASK FIRST.

Kelmscott is a most peaceful small village which lies in the south Cotswolds. The village is full of old stone buildings, the most famous of which is Kelmscott Manor. This superb building was erected in 1571 and was occupied between 1871 and 1896 by William Morris, the famous poet, artist and craftsman, who ensured that the 19th-century restoration was carefully carried out. William Morris's tombstone can be seen in the churchyard at St George's church. The family is remembered through the Memorial Cottages in the village. No 1 Memorial Gardens was paid for in 1902 by Jane Morris, the wife of the great man. No 2 Memorial Gardens was paid for by May Morris, their daughter, in 1915, in memory of her mother.

With the co-operation of local planners and the National Trust the peaceful calm of Kelmscott is assured.

This short easy stroll leads down to the River Thames and then takes you up a good farm track past Kelmscott Manor and the Memorial Cottages.

The Plough

Built in 1631, the Plough is but a short walk from Kelmscott Manor and the River Thames. You will be assured of a warm welcome.

From Monday to Saturday the pub is open from 11 am to 3 pm and from 7 pm to 11 pm, while on Sunday the hours are from 12 noon to 3 pm and 7 pm to 10.30 pm. Hook Norton, London Pride and a guest ale will always be on tap, as will Strongbow and Black Rat scrumpy cider. A wide choice of wines is available by the bottle or the glass.

Modern and traditional style British food is made of freshly cooked, quality ingredients with speciality platters on offer. The cold seafood platter and the vegetarian platter are popular with locals and visitors. Food is available throughout the week from 12 noon to 2.30 pm and from 7 pm to 9 pm. In the evening an à la carte menu applies. This is a popular pub and booking is necessary for Sunday lunch.

There is a pleasant garden area. Children under strict control are allowed in the pub. Dogs are allowed in the bar and the garden if under strict control. There is a small car park for customers. Telephone: 01367 253543.

PLACES OF INTEREST NEARBY

Kelmscott Manor is open to the public – to find out about the opening hours telephone 01367 252486.

Buscot Park and House (4 miles S) is owned by the National Trust and comprises a late 18th-century neo-classical house with superb gardens. Telephone: 01367 240786.

Great Coxwell Barn (6 miles SE) is a 13th-century monastic barn (National Trust). Telephone: 01793 762209.

The Walk

① From The Plough, go sharp left down the track at the side of the pub. As you pass by the last house, the track becomes a hedged footpath going generally west. Stroll along this path for about 200 yards and then go left to join a footpath going south, being set to the right of the field hedge. In the autumn this is pleasant walking with a crop of gold to your right – when I walked this path it was a field of oats.

In some 300 yards you will go over a double footbridge over a stream and will soon arrive on the banks of the River Thames near to a footbridge. You can go over the footbridge onto the land opposite, from where you will have a pleasant view of moored boats.

② Return to the north bank of the river and now go north-east, walking the Thames Path towards Kelmscott. If you are lucky you will see boats on the river and maybe swans and cygnets and coots all happily living together. You will also see a wartime concrete bunker. After about $^3/_4$ mile of pleasant walking you will arrive at a hand-gate.

③ Go through the hand-gate and bear left up the track towards the village. You will pass by a second concrete bunker and then will arrive on the road outside the gateway to Kelmscott Manor. Continue up the road, arcing left to progress up the main area of the village.

On your left you will pass by No 1

The River Thames

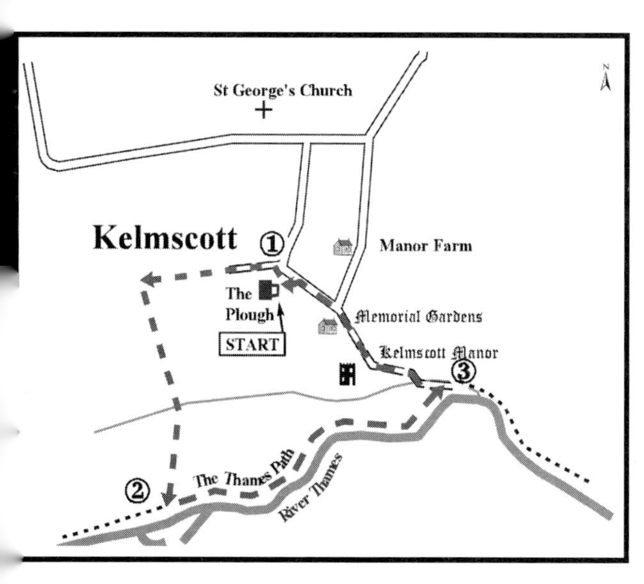

Memorial Gardens and should note the beautifully carved wall plaque on the building. This building was erected in 1902 by Jane Morris, the wife of William Morris, as a memorial to him. The carving was created by George Jack, from a drawing by Webb, and depicts William Morris reclining in Home Mead beside Kelmscott Manor. If you continue along the road you will soon be back at the Plough.

Abindgon

The Nags Head on the Thames

MAP: OS EXPLORER 170 (GR SP:499967) | WALK 22 | **DISTANCE:** $1\frac{1}{2}$ MILES

DIRECTIONS TO START: ABINGDON IS SITUATED $8\frac{1}{2}$ MILES SOUTH OF OXFORD. LEAVE OXFORD ON THE A34 AND ENTER ABINGDON VIA THE A415, THAT CROSSES OVER ABINDGON BRIDGE NEAR TO THE CAR PARK. **PARKING:** PARK IN THE PAY AND DISPLAY CAR PARK NEAR TO THE RIVER THAMES.

Abingdon means Æbbe's Hill and is probably named after an Anglo Saxon woman of royal birth. Between 1556 and 1869 Abingdon was the county town of Berkshire but in 1974 lost its borough status and became part of Oxfordshire.

For many centuries the town was dominated by a Benedictine abbey (founded in the late 7th century and said to be even larger than Westminster Abbey) but today only ruins remain.

Today the town's superb old County Hall dominates the centre of the town. It was built between 1678 and 1682 as the county assize court and market house but is now occupied by Abingdon Museum.

This easy stroll takes you along the banks of the beautiful River Thames and crosses over the weir into the town of Abingdon. From here you will stroll past the remains of the old abbey and the guildhall to arrive in the Market Place near to the impressive County Hall buildings. The route continues by the church and the superb old almshouses before you cross back over Abingdon Bridge to the pub.

The Nags Head on the Thames

This fascinating pub is in fact part of the 15th-century Abingdon Bridge (rebuilt in the 19th century) over the River Thames, being set on three islands – the river actually runs beneath the dining area of the pub. From the bridge there are splendid views over the river and the town, and the spire of St Helen's stands proud.

The pub is open between 11 am and 11 pm during the week and at weekends from 12 noon to 10.30 pm. The real ales to enjoy are Bass, Boddington's, Castle Eden and Director's, while Dry Blackthorn is the cider to try.

Monday to Thursday food is available between 12 noon and 3 pm and from 5 pm to 9 pm; on Friday and Saturday from 12 noon to 6 pm only (5 pm on Sunday). It is a special treat to dine in the patio garden above the river, where one can watch the world go by. Bar snacks vary from fish and chips to Mediterranean chicken and there is an all day carvery at the weekend, which proves very popular with locals and visitors alike.

Being situated on the river bridge, there is no car park so the nearby pay and display car park is recommended. Children are allowed in the lounge and garden but dogs, under strict control, are allowed only in the garden. Telephone: 01235 536645.

'he Walk

1) From the car park stroll down to .bingdon Bridge, join the Thames Path y walking beneath the fine bridge and roceed along the side of the River Thames, where you can expect an abundance of water craft during the summer months. In 700 yards you will arrive at Abingdon Lock.

② Cross over the river at the weir. You will walk on part of the island and then arrive on the far bank near to the old abbey grounds. Sadly there is very little of the old abbey to see. Bear left up Abbey Close to walk past The Folly and near Abbey House; then bear left between the Guildhall and St Nicholas's church to arrive in Market Place in the centre of Abingdon. Stroll to the left of the magnificent County Hall and veer right to continue along Lombard Street.

③ Go left down West St Helen's Street and you will see the old Morland Brewery building to the right. By the church building, bear left to see Twitty's Almshouses and then walk past Long Alley Almshouses and Brick Alley Almshouses. As you progress left along St Helen's Wharf there is a pleasant view over the River Thames and then you will have to bear left again to return to the town centre via East St Helen's Street. Just past County Hall, go right and walk down Bridge Street and you will soon arrive by the bridge. Keep to the left of

PLACES OF INTEREST NEARBY

Moorland Brewery (Abingdon) has been recently taken over by Greene King but the original buildings remain and can be visited by appointment. Telephone: 01235 540475.

Out and about in Abingdon – The Thames Path offers miles of wonderful walking or one can take a trip down the river by boat. Telephone: 01235 522711 (Abingdon TIC).

The River Thames

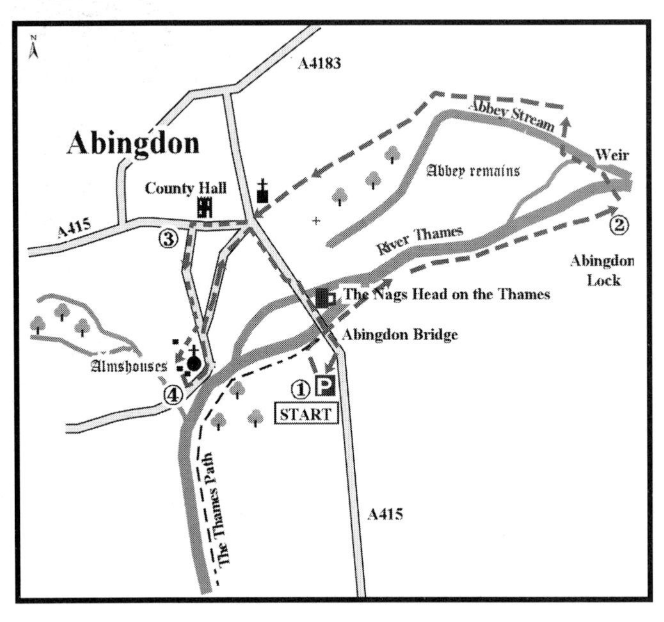

the street to have sa
passage over the bridg
You will go ove
Abbey Stream and ca
then visit the Nag
Head on the Thame
which is set overlookin
the waters of th
Thames. After passin
over the main rive
bridge, cross over th
road once again
return to the car park.

Dorchester
Fleur de Lys Inn

MAP: OS EXPLORER 170 (GR SP:578941) | **WALK 23** | **DISTANCE:** 2½ MILES

DIRECTIONS TO START: DORCHESTER IS SITUATED 8 MILES EAST OF ABINGDON. LEAVE ABINGDON ON THE A415 AND AT BURCOT TURN RIGHT ONTO THE MINOR ROAD SIGNPOSTED TO THE VILLAGE. **PARKING:** PARK IN THE FREE VILLAGE CAR PARK AT BRIDGE END. ALTERNATIVELY, CUSTOMERS MAY USE THE CAR PARK AT THE FLEUR DE LYS INN WHILE WALKING – BUT PLEASE ASK FIRST.

To visit Dorchester on a sunny day is like a day in paradise. This most beautiful small village, which is set near to the banks of the River Thames, offers a history going back to the Bronze Age. In AD 634 the Milanese missionary Birinus came to preach to the West Saxons and he founded the bishopric. Some years later, the see was transferred to Winchester, although nothing remains of the old Anglo-Saxon cathedral. Augustinian canons built the present abbey which was enlarged in the 13th and 14th centuries. The beautiful abbey is undoubtedly the main attraction to visitors, who are mesmerised by the 200 ft long building and its Jesse window surrounded by tree branches of stone enshrining the original carved figures and richly coloured glass depicting Mary's genealogy.

This fine stroll takes you along the banks of the River Thames, passing by Little Wittenham Bridge to see narrowboats and motor launches making their way along the mighty river. The return route takes you into Dorchester to stroll the superb High Street and to see the many period buildings and picturesque thatched cottages, and there is an opportunity to visit the abbey.

Fleur de Lys Inn

This historic 16th-century inn has an interesting cob wall in its car park. The inn is situated in the middle of the village, being near to the many wonderful buildings that line the High Street, and offers easy access to Dorchester Abbey. The rear garden is very nice but it is also pleasant to sit at one of the roadside tables and watch the modern world pass through history.

During the week, opening hours are from 11 am to 3 pm and 6.30 pm to 11 pm, while at the weekend the evening opening is from 7 pm to 10.30 pm. IPA, Ruddles, Old Speckled Hen and guest beers are the real ales to try and there is Blackthorn Dry for the cider drinker, plus a selection of wines.

During the week reasonably priced good pub grub is available between 12 noon and 2 pm (weekends to 3 pm) and from 6.30 pm to 11 pm (weekends from 7 pm to 10.30 pm), the lovely pies being a local favourite. On Sunday evenings in the winter food gives way to the local quiz.

Children are allowed in the inn; dogs must be kept on leads at all times when allowed in the bar and garden. Telephone: 01865 340502.

The Walk

① From the Bridge End car park go left (south) past the toilet block and the church of St Birinus, then bear right down Willenham Lane. At the end of the lane continue ahead on a footpath that leads down to the banks of the River Thames – you will go over pasture-land, passing by a stream that runs into the main river.

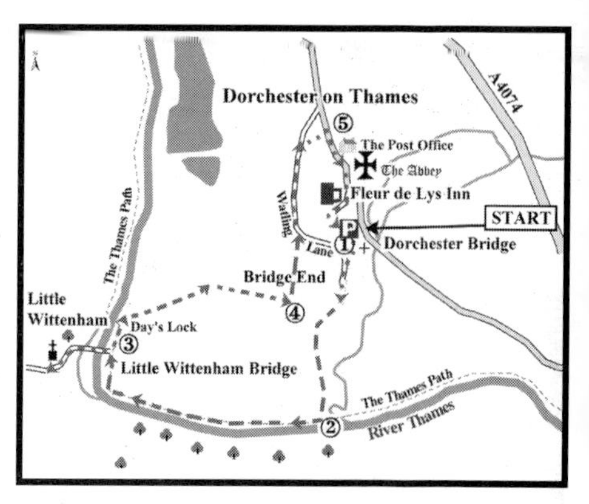

② Turn right and stroll along the Thames Path for about half a mile. This is lovely walking with the river to your left, where you may see ducks, swans, coots and moorhens or perhaps a red kite or buzzard high in the sky. Boats are likely to be on the river and as you progress around the river bend you will arrive at Little Wittenham Bridge. Take time to stroll over the bridge past the Thames Conservancy building onto the small island. You can walk on the island and will have a pleasing view of Day's Lock ahead and/or you can continue over a second bridge and stroll up a lane to see the beautiful St Peter's church in Little Wittenham. At the side of the church there is a private tower and a manor house – these are occupied as the HQ of the Northmoor Trust. Return over the island and retrace your steps over Little Wittenham Bridge.

③ Go left and continue up the Thames Path to Day's Lock. You can enter the lock area via a hand-gate and enjoy watching the superb launches and other craft making their way along the mighty Thames. When you are ready, exit via the same hand-gate and now follow the waymark post to Dorchester village. The

Day's Lock

path leads to a clear footpath, passing by some mounds with cultivated land to their left.

④ In about 400 yards, look out for a path going off to your left that leads up to the edge of bushes and houses in Dorchester village. Go up this path and soon you can bear right to arrive in the village on Watling Lane. Go left along this quiet lane for some 300 yards. You will pass by a number of attractive houses and a beautiful thatched cottage. When you reach No 19 Watling Lane, turn right up a path waymarked High Street to the centre of the village. You will pass by a further attractive thatched cottage as you arrive in the High Street of this most beautiful of villages.

⑤ Go right and stroll the superb street, taking time to enjoy the wonderful old buildings; the post office is a particularly fine one. On your left go through the lychgate to see the very fine abbey and then return to the High Street, where you will see the Fleur de Lys Inn opposite. Just past the inn, bear right to walk past yet another beautiful thatched cottage and, here, go along a footpath to the left of a lovely black and white building. This will lead you back to the car park.

PLACES OF INTEREST NEARBY

Didcot Railway Centre (8 miles S) endeavours to recreate the golden age of the Great Western train, offering a fine collection of old locomotives and carriages. Telephone: 01235 817200.

Little Wittenham nature reserve (on the walking route) comprises some 250 acres of land offering scenic views and peaceful places to enjoy. Telephone: 01865 407792.

Faringdon
The Old Crown Coaching Inn

MAP: OS EXPLORER 170 (GR SP:288954) | **WALK 24** | **DISTANCE:** 2 MILES

DIRECTIONS TO START: FARINGDON IS SITUATED 10 MILES NORTH-WEST OF WANTAGE. LEAVE WANTAGE ON THE A417 AND THIS WILL TAKE YOU INTO FARINGDON.
PARKING: SOUTHAMPTON STREET PAY AND DISPLAY CAR PARK IS NEAR TO THE TOWN CENTRE.

The attractive town of Faringdon is situated on a limestone ridge between the Ock and Thames valleys. At the time of Domesday there were but nine houses in Faringdon but it did mark the northern boundary between Mercia and Wessex for King Alfred the Great. The English Civil War brought the town to the front in historic terms. While the Parliamentarians were closing in on Oxford, Oliver Cromwell chose to attack Faringdon. He quartered his men on Folly Hill, overlooking the town, but the Royalists withdrew into Faringdon House. A siege of Elizabethan Faringdon House started on 29th April 1645 but Cromwell was held back. At the end of the war, Charles I negotiated an honourable surrender of Faringdon, which had almost been ruined by the siege. Prosperity returned in the coaching age and a thriving market returned.

This easy walk will take you up to see a folly from where there is a superb view of the surrounding area. After strolling along a good path/track through attractive countryside, you will arrive back in the town near to the rear of Faringdon House.

The Old Crown Coaching Inn

Situated in the centre of Faringdon near to the superb town hall, the Old Crown Coaching Inn is an historic inn. During the 18th century, Cotswold wool merchants, cloth traders and other weary travellers would call in on their way to London. It was the court house until 1858 and the landlord served as the post master until 1898.

The inn is open on weekdays from 11 am to 11 pm and at weekends from 12 noon to 10.30 pm, when Ruddles, Abbot and Old Speckled Hen are the real ales to savour, while Strongbow and Woodpecker ciders will please the cider drinker. There is also a wide selection of house and other wines available.

Food is available throughout the week between 12 noon and 2.30 pm and 6.30 pm to 9 pm. There is an English bar menu and an à la carte menu to select from. The chef's specials are very popular with locals and visitors alike.

There is a large garden to enjoy. Neither children nor dogs are allowed into the inn.

Telephone: 01367 242744.

The Walk

① From the car park in Southampton Street, turn right, ascend the street into Ferndale Street and eventually you will arrive at a road junction with London Street and Stanford Road. Turn right into Stanford Road and cross over to walk the footpath by the side of the Cotswold stone wall. In about 100 yards, go left up a walled tarmac footpath that leads to the Old Folly tower. This is easy walking and to your left you will see a large hotel with its golf course.

After walking the footpath for about 300 yards you will reach the open and a fine view of the Old Folly tower can be enjoyed as you progress into the trees that surround the tower. If visiting on the first Sunday of the month, you will find the tower open and you may ascend the 150+ steps to reach the viewing platform at the top for a truly magnificent view over Faringdon and the surrounding area. When ready, continue through the trees to reach the open once again. Proceed ahead (north-east) and now descend the other side of the hill towards the bushes in the coppice below.

② Immediately after strolling past the trees, go left on a clear path that will take you generally northwards along the edge of the trees. At the field end proceed over the stile onto the old London road. Cross over the road and continue along the track opposite signed 'Smokedown 2'. This good track will lead you to Grove Lodge.

③ Now go left to return to Faringdon town. This is easy walking along a fenced path, with clear views all around – you will have glimpses of the Old Folly tower up to your left, while to the right typical Oxfordshire countryside will catch your

PLACES OF INTEREST NEARBY

Great Coxwell Barn (2 miles SW) is a 13th-century monastic barn owned by the National Trust. Telephone: 01793 762209.

Buscot Park and House (4 miles W) is owned by the National Trust and comprises a late 18th-century neo-classical house and Italianate water garden. Telephone: 01367 240786.

The old town hall

eye. After about 600 yards you will pass by Church Path Farm, joining their farm lane, which will then lead you into Church Street (the A4095) on the edge of the lovely town. You will pass by the rear gateway to Faringdon House, which is hidden among the trees, and soon arrive at All Saints' church. A left turn will take you back to the centre of the town and the Old Crown Coaching Inn.

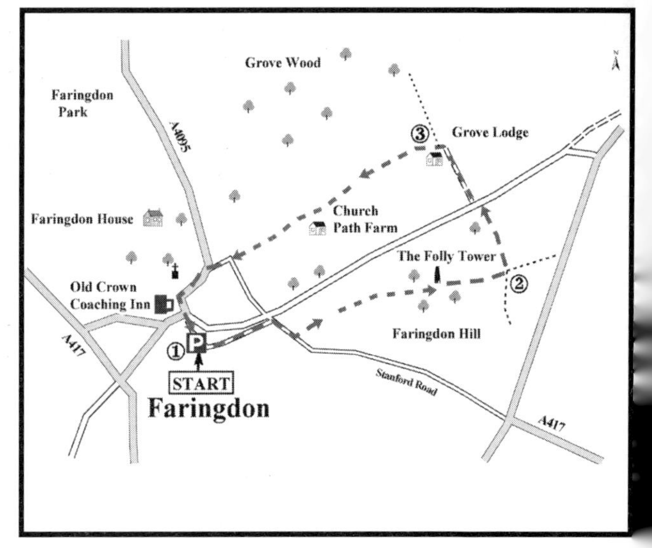

Christmas Common

The Fox & Hounds

MAP: OS EXPLORER 171 (GR SP:714932)

WALK 25

DISTANCE: 3 MILES

DIRECTIONS TO START: CHRISTMAS COMMON IS SITUATED 17 MILES SOUTH-EAST OF OXFORD. TAKE THE B480 FROM OXFORD THROUGH WATLINGTON AND HILL ROAD WILL LEAD YOU INTO CHRISTMAS COMMON. **PARKING:** CUSTOMERS MAY USE THE CAR PARK AT THE FOX AND HOUNDS WHILE WALKING – PLEASE ASK FIRST.

It was Christmas Day in 1643 when the Royalists and the Parliamentarians (the Roundheads) squared up to each other on the common land to the south of Watlington in this most scenic part of the Chiltern Hills. Even Cromwell wanted a rest and it was decided to have a truce. As a result, the local area became known as Christmas Common.

The common is very rural indeed, with very few houses. The 1811 census indicated that there were only six inhabited houses at that time but today this has risen to nearly fifty houses. The area is generally hilly, with lovely woodland. Watlington House is the only major house in the area and this is well hidden among the trees.

This lovely stroll takes you through attractive woodland near to Watlington House, and there is a very fine view for you to enjoy as you descend Watlington Hill to the B480 road. The route continues into open country along the peaceful Hill Road, with yet more good views over nearby Pyrton Hill, before you join the Oxfordshire Way back to Christmas Common.

The Fox and Hounds

The old pub dates back to the 16th century but it was not until 1896 that Brakspear's acquired the property for Rom Greys Brewery. This is a friendly pub, where the very best food is offered.

It is open from 11.30 am to 11 pm during the week and at weekends from 11 am to 10.30 pm – being situated in the countryside opening hours can vary during the winter months. A good selection of Brakspear real ales dominates, while Thatcher's ciders are a special treat for the cider drinker.

A superb wine list complements the fine food that is available. Between 12 noon and 2.30 pm a bar menu is offered and usually includes steak pie. In the evenings, the ribeye steak is a local favourite, and who could resist the chocolate and Guinness tart? The food is generally modern British using organic and local fare and has been known to attract a national celebrity or two.

There is a pleasant garden area where children are allowed. Dogs on leads and under strict control are allowed in the bar and the garden. Telephone: 01491 612599.

The Walk

① From the pub car park, turn right along the verge of the road for about 100 yards. Immediately after passing by End Lodge, turn right up a driveway past the lodge and continue into woodland. After about 100 yards, bear right and continue into the attractive woodland, where bluebells form a carpet of blue in the spring. As you proceed through the woodland the path arcs left into Lower Dean Wood (NT) and you may be lucky enough to see deer shyly disappearing into the trees. After exiting the woodland a fine view opens out to your right and you walk a meadow path along the top of the hill. You will be able to see Wallingford to the right and will enjoy a brief glimpse of Watlington House behind you.

② After walking along the top of the meadow for about 200 yards, go right and commence a steep descent through the meadowland – in summer the wild flowers add to the fine view ahead of you. When you reach the bottom of the meadow, proceed over a further stile through the end of a small wood and then walk the good track that leads to the B480, Howe Road. At the road, go right and walk its verge for about 300 yards.

③ At a junction of roads/tracks, turn right along the waymarked Ridgeway track. Stroll along this hedged track for almost ¾ mile and you will have pleasing glimpses of Watlington Hill to the right. Just after passing the entrance to a small caravan site you will reach a road. Cross over the road with care and look for a hand-gate set up to the right. Go through this hand-gate and cross over some wasteland on a clear path going generally north. At the end of the wasteland proceed ahead on a footpath through scrub land.

PLACES OF INTEREST NEARBY

Wallingford (9 miles SW) is an historic town that was granted its charter in 1155. Information from Wallingford Tourist Information Centre. Telephone: 01491 826972.

On the walk

④ The path gently arcs to the right and in about 400 yards you will be clear of the small trees and can enjoy a fine view over Pyrton Hill to the left. The final stretch of the path hugs the top of the hill and the hedge-line as it nears the buildings of Watlington Hill Farm, which you will see up to your right. All too soon you will go over a stile to join the Oxfordshire Way (coming in from your left). Walk the clear route over a final stile and you will arrive on the road that leads back to the pub.

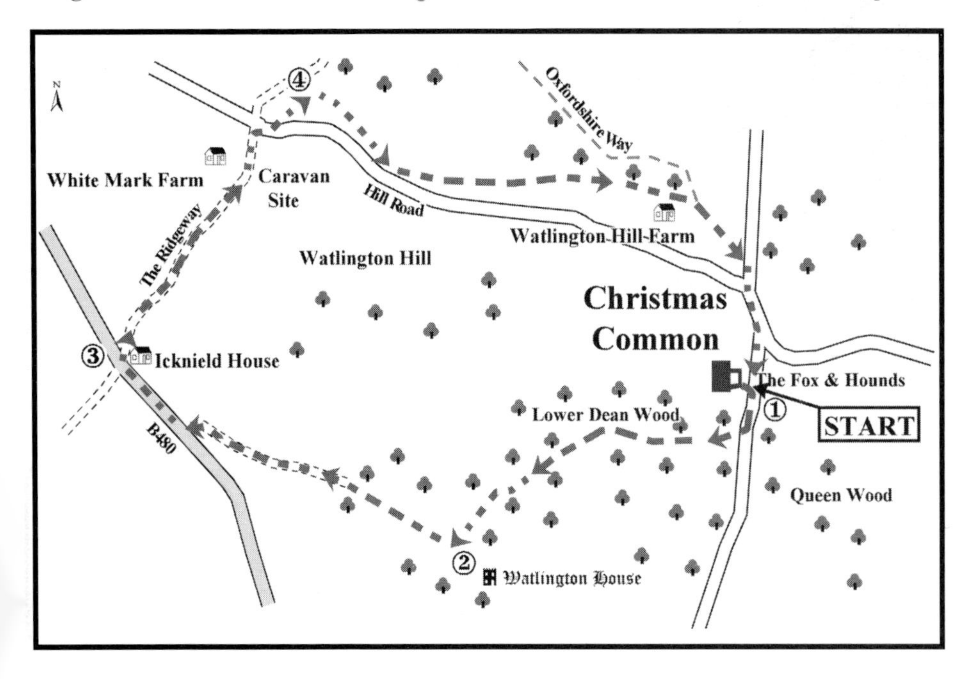

Wallingford
The Boathouse

MAP: OS EXPLORER 170 (GR SP:611894) | **WALK 26** | **DISTANCE:** $2\frac{1}{2}$ MILES

DIRECTIONS TO START: WALLINGFORD IS 12 MILES SOUTH-EAST OF ABINGDON. LEAVE ABINGDON ON THE A415. TURN RIGHT AT THE A4074 JUNCTION AND FOLLOW THE A4074 TOWARDS WALLINGFORD. ABOUT 1 MILE AFTER PASSING THROUGH BENSON, GO LEFT INTO THE TOWN OF WALLINGFORD. **PARKING:** PARK IN THE MUNICIPAL CAR PARK BY THE SWIMMING POOL ON THE FAR SIDE OF WALLINGFORD BRIDGE.

Historic Wallingford was founded by King Alfred in the 10th century and still has some impressive earthworks and fortifications. By 1066, it was the leading town in Berkshire and housed the Royal Mint. After his victory at Hastings, William the Conqueror arrived and ordered a royal castle to be built. During the Civil War, the castle was held under siege by Oliver Cromwell. After a long twelve weeks the castle was forced to surrender and Cromwell ordered its demolition in 1652.

Today, Wallingford is a most attractive town and it is a pleasure to stroll along the banks of the River Thames and to meander around the back streets, which still reflect its ancient origins.

This fine walk takes you along the bank of the River Thames and there are fine views of the lovely Wallingford Bridge. On the return route you will stroll along the footpath on the opposite bank of the River and enter Wallingford town, passing the town hall. The stroll ends near to the Boathouse where refreshments await.

The Boathouse

The Boathouse straddles an ancient ford in the River Thames and offers outstanding views over the longest lock-free stretch of the famous river. What a pleasure it is to sit near to the famous Wallingford Bridge on one of the outside tables and watch the sailing world go by.

The inn is open all day every day between 12 noon and 11 pm, when a wide selection of real ales is available. Strongbow will attract the cider drinker and there is a large selection of wines for the connoisseur of the grape. Food is available between 12 noon and 8 pm, when one can select from the traditional menu of light snacks or go for a hearty meal.

There is a super garden/patio overlooking the river and children are allowed in the bar and the garden. Dogs are restricted to the garden/patio and must be kept on their lead and under control at all times.

Telephone: 01491 834100.
Website: www.theboathouse.net
E-mail: raycody@hotmail.com

The Walk

① From the car park walk down to the side of the impressive River Thames and proceed through the gateway beneath the Wallingford Bridge to join the Thames Path. Walk along the path for about ½ mile. From the river bank you will enjoy a pleasing view of the beautiful bridge with the superb steeple of St Peter's church adding to the scene. After passing through a second gateway you will see Newnham Farm ahead of you. As you approach the farm, look out for a path line to take you to the left of the farm buildings onto a farm track. Proceed right along this track between the buildings, maintaining a southerly direction, and continue ahead along a hedged path passing by the buildings of the International Commonwealth Agricultural Bureau (on your left) until you arrive at the A4130.

② Turn right along the footpath over the Thames and then go right again to descend to the Thames Path once again, now on the west bank of the river. As you walk along the clear path you will go over a footbridge over Bradford Brook. Note the 1913 Thames Conservancy building, on which you may see that there are flood marks indicating the flood levels of 1897, 1947 and 1979. As you continue towards Wallingford you will walk at the back of

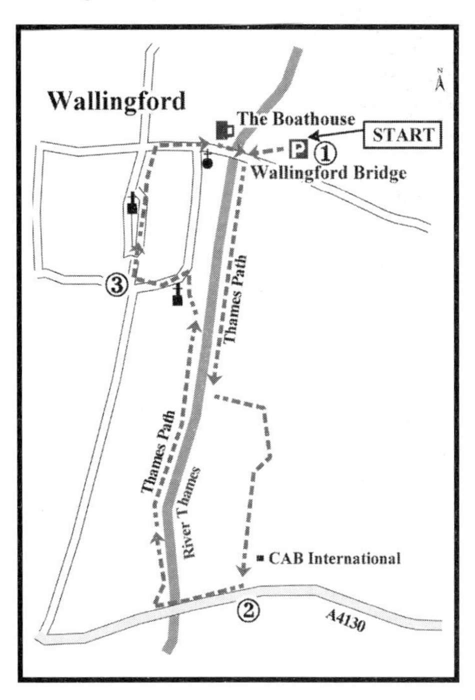

The pub's riverside garden

some attractive houses which all have their own landing stage. As you progress you will see that a number of these have a wide concrete area to the left of the footpath and then as you reach the open space again you will realise that many years ago this was all part of an airstrip for light aircraft.

Continue along the hedge-lined path and soon you will emerge on a lane that arcs left. At the corner, turn right through a passageway under a house and proceed over a stream, noting the lovely black and white building to the left. As you progress up the path, St Leonard's church will be on your left and you will arrive in the front of the church. If you have time, stroll around the churchyard, which is a conservation area; you will find a number of interesting plants with labels of identification. Continue up St Leonard's Lane until you reach St Mary's Street.

③ Turn right along St Mary's Street until you arrive in the market square where you can visit St Mary Le More church and take time to see the town hall, in which the Tourist Information Office is situated. Note the sign which records the 800th anniversary of the town (1155 to 1955). Continue along St Mary's Street, then turn right along the interesting old High Street until you arrive near to Wallingford Bridge. The entrance to the Boathouse is on the left just before you reach Wallingford Bridge.

PLACES OF INTEREST NEARBY

Didcot Railway Centre (8 miles S) endeavours to recreate the golden age of the Great Western steam train, offering a fine collection of old locomotives and carriages. Telephone: 01235 817200.

Wellplace Zoo, Ipsden ($4\frac{1}{2}$ miles SE) offers a large collecton of birds and animals from all over the world. Telephone: 01491 680473.

East Hendred
The Wheatsheaf Inn

MAP: OS **EXPLORER 170 (GR SP:459889)** | **WALK 27** | **DISTANCE:** 4 MILES

DIRECTIONS TO START: EAST HENDRED IS 5 MILES EAST OF WANTAGE, BEING SITUATED JUST OFF THE A417. **PARKING:** CUSTOMERS MAY USE THE CAR PARK AT THE WHEATSHEAF INN WHILE WALKING – PLEASE ASK FIRST.

After the Norman Conquest many small villages were divided between the Norman knights and abbots and the village of Hendred was one of these, being divided into five manors. East Hendred is a by-product and today it is now a peaceful picturesque village surrounded by farms and orchards. Hendred House has been occupied by the Eyston family since 1453 – they were related by marriage to Sir Thomas More, the Chancellor to Henry VIII. Near to the Wheatsheaf Inn is the chapel of Jesus of Bethlehem (now a museum), which, together with its priest's cottage, formed the centre of the village.

The stroll takes you past this and the fascinating church of St Augustine, which, built by the Eyston family in 1858, has a 'faceless' clock and a unique crusader lectern. You will also visit the attractive villages of East and West Hendred, along good footpaths and farm tracks. So, enjoy the fine views and admire the lovely buildings.

The Wheatsheaf Inn

The Wheatsheaf Inn is a friendly, family inn, once a coaching inn, that dates back to the 16th century. It is a pleasure to sit in the front garden and enjoy a snack or pint in the lovely village of East Hendred.

The inn is open from 12 noon to 3 pm and from 6 pm to 11 pm during the week. On Saturday it is open all day between 12 noon and 11 pm, while on Sunday the opening hours are between 12 noon and 10.30 pm. IPA and Abbot are the two main real ales on tap but there is always a guest ale. Perhaps the Strongbow cider is your tipple or you may prefer to select from the wide range of wines by the glass or by the bottle.

Food is available from 12 noon to 2 pm each day of the week. From Monday to Saturday you can get food in the evenings between 6.30 pm and 9 pm. It is advisable to book for the Sunday roast, but no food is served on Sunday evenings. You can select from a full bar snack menu or indulge yourself with a full meal. There is always a specials board with many tasty courses to enjoy – the homemade pies are a favourite with many of the locals.

There is a pleasant garden area at the rear of the inn. Children and dogs are allowed in the inn – dogs must always be kept on their lead. Telephone: 01235 833229.

The Walk

① From the car park at the inn, bear left down Chapel Square and then turn right along the High Street of this attractive village, past the Eyston Arms pub. Shortly after passing by the superb old post office building, go left along a lane that takes you to the left of Hendred House. Soon you will arrive in woodland and after about 200 yards you will reach the end of the trees on your left.

② Go down a wide track to the right and descend through the trees in a generally south-west direction. At the bottom of the slope, go initially left, then right up a clear track to the left of a wire fence. Soon this track arcs left and you will be in open countryside. To your right you will enjoy a fine view over East Hendred. The track now curves right (south-east) and you will arrive at a junction of tracks by some trees.

③ Proceed right and walk the good track by the right edge of the trees and in about 300 yards you will reach a lane. Proceed ahead along this lane and continue over the road, now with the trees on your right. This clear track aims generally west and when you have left the trees behind there are some lovely views to your right.

④ Some 600 yards after leaving the trees you will reach a road, where you go right. Descend the road and you will pass by Ginge Road Cottages on the way into West Hendred. At the road junction you

PLACES OF INTEREST NEARBY

Didcot Railway Centre (8 miles S) endeavours to recreate the golden age of the Great Western steam train, offering a fine collection of old locomotives and carriages. Telephone: 01235 817200.

Vale and Downland Museum, Wantage (5 miles E) – a community centre museum housed in a 17th-century cloth merchant's house. Telephone: 01235 771447.

The village post office

can stop to see the lovely thatched corner cottage and can stroll down the lane to visit Holy Trinity church. Continue into the village.

⑤ Where the road bends left, go right, then left onto a clear tarmac footpath that takes you along the back of attractive houses. The path arcs left and then right as it proceeds between cultivated fields to arrive in East Hendred at a road junction near to the school. Cross over the road and stroll ahead along Church Street. Pause to visit the church of St Augustine of Canterbury.

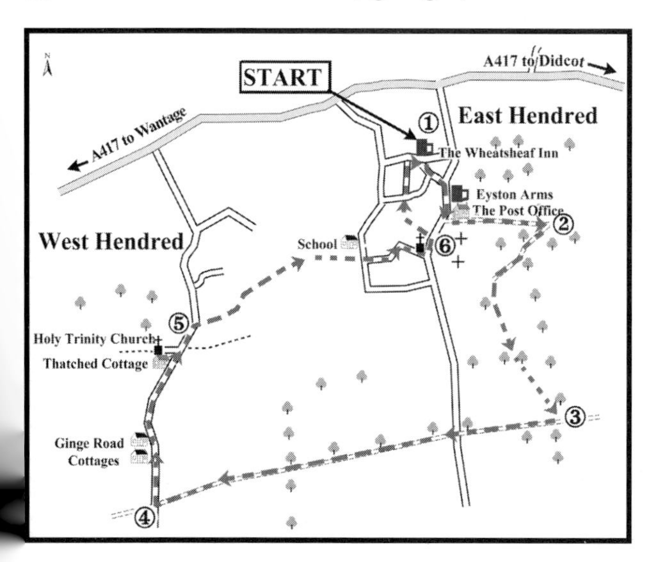

⑥ Continue by going left along the High Street, then in about 100 yards, go left again up a signed footpath along a lovely green path that leads towards the village cemetery. Proceed into Cat Street. Go right to return to Chapel Square and the Wheatsheaf Inn.

Woolstone
The White Horse

MAP: OS EXPLORER 170 (GR SP:294878) WALK 28 **DISTANCE:** 4 MILES

DIRECTIONS TO START: WOOLSTONE IS SITUATED ABOUT 1 MILE SOUTH-WEST OF UFFINGTON AND 6 MILES SOUTH OF FARINGDON. FROM UFFINGTON THE WOOLSTONE ROAD LEADS DIRECTLY INTO THE VILLAGE. **PARKING:** CUSTOMERS MAY USE THE CAR PARK AT THE WHITE HORSE WHILE WALKING – PLEASE ASK FIRST.

The Uffington hill figure – the White Horse – is set in breathtaking scenery and marks a mysterious pagan past. It is the oldest chalk figure in Britain and the landscape has inspired numerous painters, poets and musicians over the years and today. Measuring 360ft by 126ft, the amazing White Horse is the second largest figure in Britain. Dragon Hill is the flat topped hillock known by many as The Castle, and local myth suggests that this is where St George slew the dragon. The Ridgeway path crosses the hills near to the White Horse, and Waylands Smithy ($1^1/_4$ miles westwards along the Ridgeway) is a 5,000-year-old prehistoric tomb.

After an inspirational stroll along the top of the hill you can walk a permissive path down towards the village of Woolstone. The National Trust, which is responsible for the care and maintenance of this wonderful piece of heritage, has owned White Horse Hill since 1979.

The White Horse

Situated in the peaceful village of Woolstone, The White Horse was built around 1540 and is full of interest and character.

From Monday to Saturday opening hours are between 11 am (12 noon on Sunday) and 3 pm and 6 pm to 11 pm (7 pm to 10.30 pm on Sundays), when Akle, Hook Norton and guest ales are the real ales on offer, while Scrumpy Jack and Blackthorn Dry will please the cider drinkers.

Food is available between 11 am (12 noon on Sundays) and 3 pm and from 6 pm to 10 pm (7 pm to 10.30 pm on Sundays). A full bar menu as well as an à la carte menu offer a wide selection of appetising foods and it is a delight to eat out in the attractive garden on a sunny day.

Children are allowed in the inn but dogs are not permitted. Telephone: 01367 820726.

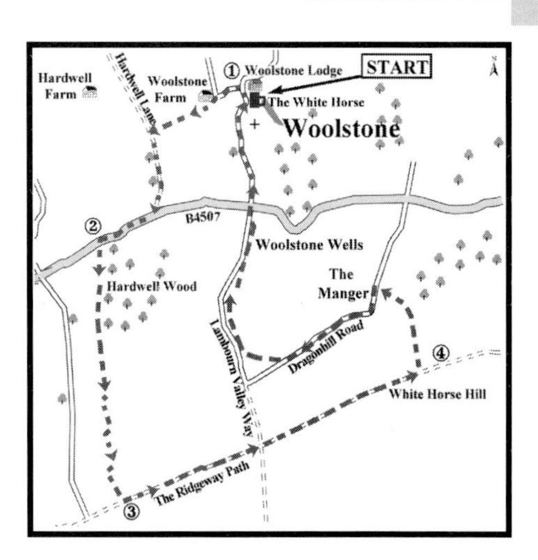

The Walk

① From the pub car park turn right and walk the pleasant lane going west past attractive houses. At the lane end follow the direction of the waymarker and go over the stile by the farm gate, then walk the footpath along the left edge of the next two fields until you reach Hardwell Lane (a hedged track). Here, go left and walk this track up to the B4507 road, then go right and walk along the edge of the generally quiet road for about 300 yards until you are by Hardwell Wood.

② Towards the end of the wood, cross over the road and proceed up the waymarked footpath into the trees. There follows a 50 yard ascent as you progress up the clear path – on a hot sunny day the shelter from the sun will be welcome. As you exit from the trees you will enjoy a fine view towards White Horse Hill. Continue ahead on the clear path over cultivated land to reach the Ridgeway Path through a hedge.

③ Go left up the Ridgeway Path taking time to enjoy the pleasing view all around you. The Ridgeway Path is in fact a good wide track but there is a side footpath available if you prefer. Walk this path for the next mile. You will ascend once again until you reach the top of the hill (go past the footpaths to the left), where you may wish to stroll up to the trig point at 850 ft. Continue along the track and there is a view of the massive cooling towers at the power station at Didcot. As the track begins to descend look out for a waymarker pointing to the left.

④ Go left along this path by a wire fence (to your right). Where the path descends left between hillocks you can enjoy a

The Manger

lovely view of The Castle (640 ft). Descend to the lane by The Castle viewing point – you can climb the steps onto the top of this to enjoy a good view of the surrounding countryside. Go left up the lane and on your right you will enjoy the superb view into The Manger, a steep-sided valley where the White Horse is alleged to rest at night. The view opens up once more as you gain height and then you turn right through a hand-gate onto National Trust land and walk the footpath towards the car park on Woolstone Hill. Unless you wish to obtain more literature from the NT mobile office, turn right before the NT hand-gate and commence a descent of the hill, keeping to the permissive path to the right of the field hedge. This leads down to a further hand-gate near to the B4507. Descend to the road and cross over to walk the lane opposite into Woolstone village. This generally quiet lane will take you past some attractive thatched cottages (note the old fire mark above the door on the first of these) and all too soon you will be back at the White Horse inn.

PLACES OF INTEREST NEARBY

The Vale and Downland Museum, Wantage (8 miles E). A country museum that illustrates the heritage of the Vale of the White Horse. Telephone: 01235 771447.

Royal Wantage (8 miles E) is an attractive small town, proud of its Roman history, and was the home of John Betjeman for some 20 years. Tourist information telephone: 01235 760176.

Rotherfield Greys

The Maltsters Arms

MAP: OS EXPLORER 171 (GR SP:725823) | WALK 29 | **DISTANCE:** 3½ MILES

DIRECTIONS TO START: ROTHERFIELD GREYS IS 3 MILES WEST OF HENLEY-ON-THAMES. LEAVE HENLEY-ON-THAMES ON THE A4155. GO RIGHT ALONG ST MARK'S ROAD AND CONTINUE WEST ALONG THE GREYS ROAD TOWARDS GREYS GREEN. AT THE ROAD JUNCTION, GO LEFT AND FOLLOW THE SIGNS INTO ROTHERFIELD GREYS. THE MALTSTERS ARMS IS ON THE RIGHT NEXT TO THE CHURCH. **PARKING:** CUSTOMERS MAY USE THE CAR PARK AT THE MALTSTERS ARMS WHILE WALKING – PLEASE ASK FIRST.

In spite of its proximity to the busy town of Henley-on-Thames, Rotherfield Greys remains a peaceful haven where beautiful cherry blossom attracts visitors in the spring and where cricket matches on the village green take one back to a former time.

St Nicholas' church is set next to the Maltsters Arms pub and serves the parishes of Rotherfield Greys and Rotherfield Peppard. Inside the church is the 1605 Knollys' tomb, which shows reclining effigies of Sir Francis Knollys and his wife Katherine plus their 16 children. The estate of Greys Court was given to the Knollys family after the battle of Bosworth. The estate eventually passed on to the Stapleton family at a time when it covered some 8,000 acres of woodland, parkland and farmland.

This easy stroll will take you from the Maltsters Arms across pastureland and cultivated fields. You will then descend a gentle hedged path, from where you will enjoy brief glimpses of Henley-on-Thames and the valley to the left. The return route is along the valley and through fields full of wild flowers before you climb back to the road near the pub.

The Maltsters Arms

Situated in the quaint village of Rotherfield Greys, next to St Nicholas' church, the Maltsters Arms is a pub that is popular with locals and visitors alike.

It is open throughout the week from 11.30 am to 3 pm and from 6 pm to 11 pm, when Brakspear's ales dominate the mind of the beer drinker, while Strongbow cider will attract the cider drinker. There is a wide selection of wines available.

Food is served between 12 noon and 2.30 pm and from 6.30 pm to 9.30 pm. A wide menu of bar snacks and full meals is available. Who could resist a chicken crepe or a slow roasted half shoulder of lamb? Sunday booking is essential at this popular eating house.

The pub has an inviting garden; children and dogs (under strict control) are allowed into the pub. Telephone: 01491 628400.

PLACES OF INTEREST NEARBY

Greys Court (1 mile N) is an estate of 300 acres of parkland surrounding the picturesque 16th-century house of the de Grey family – it is the home of Lady Brunner and is a National Trust property. Telephone: 01491 628529.

River and Rowing Museum, Henley-on-Thames (3 miles E) offers an opportunity to learn about the Thames and to experience the thrills of rowing. Telephone: 01491 415600.

The Walk

① From the car park, turn right and proceed beside the house next to the pub and walk past the village church, going over a stile into a cultivated field. Stroll along the clear path across the field, going generally south-west You will go over a couple of stiles to reach a hedged track, where you go left and walk down to Dog Lane. Cross over the lane and continue along the track opposite for 100 yards.

② Turn left down the driveway to a house called Crosslanes, exiting the garden via the hand-gate at its rear and aiming for a waymarked stile in the hedge opposite to arrive on a lane. Turn right along the lane for about 200 yards and then, just past Silgrove House, go right over a pair of stiles to arrive in a large cultivated field. Now walk along the clear path – going generally north-east to reach and go over a

Walking the farm tracks

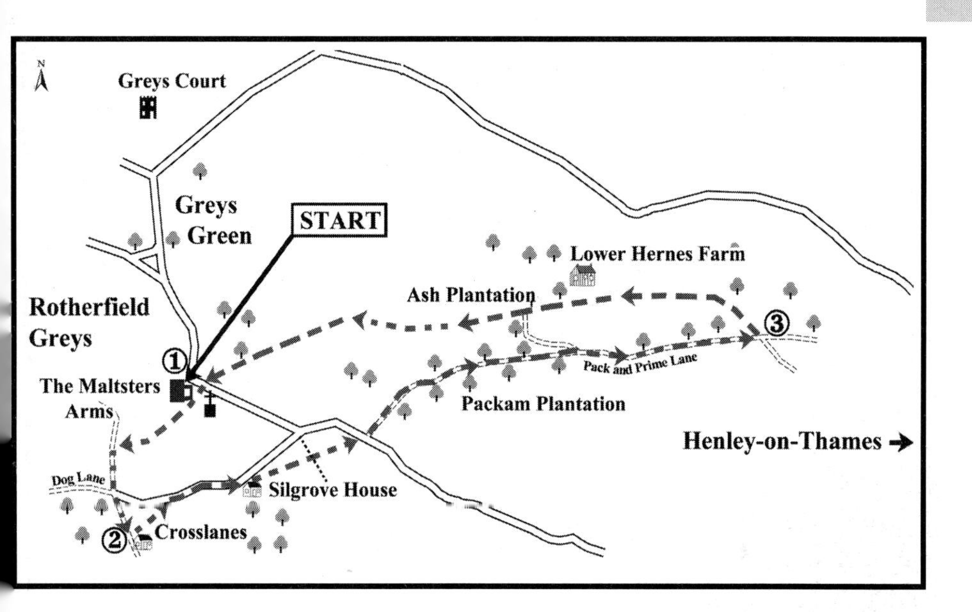

stile onto a road verge. Cross over the road and walk along the track opposite. This becomes a hedged track and you will enjoy pleasing views of the valley to your left as you progress. The track descends gently for the next $1\frac{1}{2}$ miles.

③ At a junction of paths, go left over a stile into open meadowland and walk the clear path that soon arcs generally west. This is a lovely valley path with pleasing views all round and with a mass of wild flowers in summer for you to enjoy.

You will pass by Lower Hernes Farm complex, going through a small, attractive stretch of woodland by Ash Plantation; then continue along a farm track to the left of the field hedge. A stile will take you to the right of the hedge for about 400 yards and then you return to the left of the hedge before ascending by a fence up towards Rotherfield Greys village.

A final stile will take you onto the road by the old bus shelter. Go right along the grass verge back to the Maltsters Arms pub.

Goring Heath
The King Charles Head

MAP: OS EXPLORER 171 (GR SP:664788) | WALK 30 | **DISTANCE:** 4 MILES

DIRECTIONS TO START: GORING HEATH IS SITUATED ABOUT $5\frac{1}{2}$ MILES NORTH-WEST OF READING. LEAVE READING ON THE A4074. AT CHAZEY HEATH, GO LEFT THROUGH TRENCH GREEN AND CROSS LANES TO REACH THE PUB. **PARKING:** CUSTOMERS MAY USE THE CAR PARK AT THE KING CHARLES HEAD WHILE WALKING – PLEASE ASK FIRST.

Don't forget to take your camera on this lovely stroll through attractive woodland to the picturesque village of Mapledurham. There are many beautiful cottages and almshouses lining the road into the village. Mapledurham House is an Elizabethan manor house set by the side of the River Thames. It was built by Sir Michael Blount. The estate was the setting for the film *The Eagle has Landed* and has also featured in the Inspector Morse TV series. The 14th-century church has some fine monuments to the Blounts and its oak-timbered, arcaded ceiling is particularly rare. The early-17th-century almshouses were built by John Lister.

Spare time to visit the superb watermill and to stroll around the small Mill Island for a special treat – river cruises can be booked from here.

The return route takes you past Harwick House and up through more fine woodland to arrive back at the King Charles Head for refreshments.

The King Charles Head

This historic pub dates back some 400 years and is reputed to have been used by King Charles I. Its rural setting by the roadside amid attractive woodland makes this a special place to visit and offers the opportunity for a delightful walk to Mapledurham.

From Monday to Saturday, the pub is open from 11.30 am to 3 pm and 5.30 pm to 11 pm and is open all day on Sundays between 12 noon to 10.30 pm. The real ales on offer are Badger and Tanglefoot plus various guest ales. Blackthorn Dry will appeal to the cider drinker and there is a wide selection of wines, which can be had by the bottle or by the glass. From Monday to Saturday, food is available between 12 noon and 2.30 pm and from 6 pm to 9 pm, while on Sunday it is available between 12 noon and 9 pm. There is a large, reasonably priced menu of English and European home-cooked food, and items from the Thai menu can be cooked to order. Booking for Sunday lunch is essential.

The large garden is an ideal place to relax – a real treat. Children are allowed in the pub but dogs are not. Telephone: 01491 680268.

The Walk

① From the pub car park, cross over the oad and go over the stile opposite into rassland and walk to the far corner to a econd stile. At a junction of paths turn ight over a further stile and walk the clear ath to the right of Coxsetters Wood, rossing the lovely Collingen Common. A urther stile leads onto a track and soon ou will arrive at a lane.

PLACES OF INTEREST NEARBY

Mapledurham House is a real treat. A half-day visit should be considered for this is too good to rush. Further information is available from the estate office. Telephone: 0118 9723350. Website: www.mapledurham.co.uk

② Go left down the lane towards Holly Copse. As you progress down the lane you will pass by Briar Cottage and then go down a fine bridle-path set to the immediate right of a superb black and white thatched cottage (Holly Copse Cottage). This path descends into Long Grounds Plantation, through the trees and along a laurel avenue. When you reach a junction of paths, bear left onto a track that leads you down to the edge of the plantation, which you exit via a hand-gate.

③ Walk the clear footpath set to the left of the field hedge, going in a generally south-east direction. This is delightful walking and if you are lucky you may see red kites circling overhead. Proceed past the trees of Bottom Shaw and continue past Bottom Farm, walking the farm drive down to a road. At the road, go right and stroll past The White House into the tiny village of Mapledurham.

④ When you are ready, retrace your steps back up the road to the junction and The White House, then go left along a clear wide track, walking in a north-westerly direction. Walk this track for about a mile. You will enjoy a fine view over the River Thames and soon will pass the lodge gates to Hardwick House. As you continue you will pass by the main entrance area to the house.

Mapledurham Mill

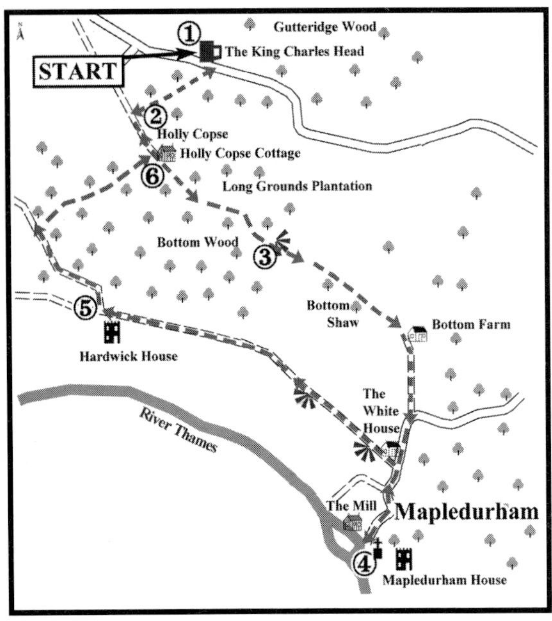

⑤ About 250 yards beyond the main building, turn right up a track that ascends steeply into Bottom Wood. Walk up this track for some 600 yards. The track arcs left, and then you will proceed through the trees until you reach a junction of tracks near to a small Christmas-tree plantation. Turn right and continue now in a generally north-easterly direction. After walking this path for about 650 yards you will arrive at a stile that leads onto the lane near to Briar Cottage.

⑥ Go left up the lane and then right to retrace your steps to the King Charles Head pub.